THE 7 FIGURE AGENCY ROADMAP

HOW TO BUILD
A MILLION DOLLAR
DIGITAL MARKETING AGENCY

JOSH NELSON
FOREWORD BY RYAN DEISS

BONUS OFFER

Thank you so much for purchasing your copy of The Seven Figure Agency Roadmap. If you are anything like me, you are much more of a visual/auditory learner.

With that in mind, I have recorded a deep dive training video that walks you through the key elements/components of the book. To access the video based version of this training please go to:

https://sevenfigureagency.com/roadmap-implementation-program

FOREWORD

by Ryan Deiss

Building an agency is hard. Prospects are jaded, existing clients are demanding, and skilled help is nearly impossible to find. And then there's the work, itself. Algorithms shift, channels come and go, and tactics that work one day become obsolete the next. At DigitalMarketer.com, it's our business to stay up to date on these trends, and even we have a hard time keeping up, so it's no wonder that many agency owners fall behind.

Fortunately, Josh Nelson discovered a better way.

As a long-time member of DigitalMarketer and a member of our Certified Partner community, Josh has studied the game, built the skills, and outlined a straightforward plan that allowed him to build a successful, 7-figure agency.

In other words, Josh is a DOER, and not merely a teacher.

Josh has applied his plan, day in and day out, on his own agency, and the result: a rapid growing, profitable agency that seems to find its way onto the Inc 5000 list of the fastest growing companies each and every year. (And if you know anything about this list, making it once is an incredible achievement, but making it multiple years in a row is truly exceptional.)

This "do then teach" mindset is what we're all about at DigitalMarketer, and it's what makes this book unusually valuable.

And when I say this book is "unusually valuable" I mean it.

In the **Seven Figure Agency Roadmap**, Josh tells you, step-by-step, how to implement your own agency marketing, how to get results for your clients, and how to implement systems so they stick around long-term. He also shows you how to build teams and systems, so you become the owner of a reliable and scalable business that can work without you. And in what will likely be your favorite part of the book, Josh opens his "black book" and tells you his preferred service providers who help him outsource the services that deliver great results for his clients, making it possible to scale your services without scaling your overhead.

In other words, this is a book about strategies and shortcuts, but mostly, this is a book about freedom. Freedom for you, and freedom for the businesses you serve.

I'm proud to recommend this book, because it's a book that needed to be written. And now that it has been written, it's a book that needs to be read and implemented.

So let's do that, shall we? Let's start building your own Seven Figure Agency Roadmap.

—RYAN DEISS
Co-Founder & CEO of DigitalMarketer

Josh teaches from his direct example of how to build a local digital marketing agency, step-by-step. I've seen few—among many-- that have the credibility, experience, and heart to truly help people build a successful agency. Service businesses is where the opportunity is for agencies and I admire Josh practicing what he preaches, going out of his way to help the rest of us.

—DENNIS YU
BlitzMetrics

I've been fortunate to be able to watch Josh drive the growth of his agency and establish their leadership in their market. He has executed as well as anyone in this industry. My advice to Agency owners: Read his book. Attend his events. Soak up everything he has to say!

—MIKE COOCH
LVRG Ventures

Josh nails it.
This book is wonderfully actionable—I challenge you to read it & not implement the frameworks he lays out in detail. It might be "The Rule of Five Ones" or his Money-Impact-Freedom model or (my favourite) delivering consistent value in exchange for recurring revenue. I've known Josh for years, he's generous with his knowledge & a whip-smart operator. Follow his advice, put in the work & you'll hit your goals.

—MIKE RHODES
Web Savvy & Agency Savvy

Josh Nelson is the real deal if you want to succeed I recommend you learn everything you can from him.

—CHRIS WINTERS
Kallzu

I've owned 2 agencies in my career, both 7 Figures. Agency 1 operated on razor thin margins and was a nightmare to run. Demanding clients required lots of sleepless nights at the office under the desk, using a pizza box as a pillow. I closed it down in under 3 years under a mountain of debt. Agency 2 operated at 30-40% profit margins, was fun as heck to run, and allowed me to spend time with my family every day while getting my clients meaningful results at the same time. I sold Agency 2 earlier this year after 22 months of operation. Night and day difference. Josh's book contains the exact step by step playbook his 7 figure agency uses every day. His methods aren't theory—they're proven. With this book you can skip all the trial and errors I made in Agency 1 and get all the benefits of Agency 2 right out the gates. It's easily worth $100 just for the first 2 chapters alone. I wish this book was written 10 years ago! I'd have slept on a lot fewer pizza boxes.

—ROBB BAILEY
Agency Alchemy

If you want a blueprint on how to create a scalable agency business, Josh is your dude. So many gurus say that they'll help you build a 7-figure agency, but few have actually done it. Josh packed his journey from struggling marketing firm to a profitable agency in this awesome resource. This book gives a step by step action plan on how to get a steady flow of clients, create a scalable business model, and retain your monthly revenue. As an agency owner and agency coach I refer everyone I come in contact to Josh. No fluff, no BS, just actionable steps to build a 7-figure agency. He literally gives you the exact model to attract clients, to close them on long-term retainers, and the SPECIFIC offers they provide per price point. As a 7-figure agency owner myself, this made me re-evaluate a few of our offers. He truly shows you how to provide exceptional value, and keep clients ready to pay you every month!

—JEFF J HUNTER
Branded Media

 Right now in the marketing world there seems to be a new model. Create a service business. Have modest success for 3-6 months. Start an advice business based on your "proof story" of your modest success. Sell as many suckers as you can. Oh and stop the service business as fast as possible because that is too close to "real work". In the agency training space, this is literally what about 90% of the "gurus" out there have done. It is weird that they are so bullish on agency but don't run an agency themselves anymore... maybe a red flag lol. Anywho... Josh Nelson is not one of those guys. He built a real multiple 7 figure agency. From the ground up. Still runs it every day. It's a non-sexy... bread and butter type agency. You know, the kind that makes you rich if you stick at it. So, when I found out Josh had written a book about his path—I just skipped straight to the buy now button and devoured it fast. If you're in an agency business and want to grow it, you should get this book. the chapter on productizing your service is more than worth the price of the whole book alone. Great advice all throughout the book. Just get it. You won't regret it.

—KEVIN HUTTO
Clients Every Day

CONTENTS

To my beautiful wife Yesenia and my two sons Brandon & Ryan. I love you! Thank you for your support of this work & your unconditional love.

"You will get all you want in life, if you help enough other people get what they want."

ZIG ZIGLAR

PREFACE

After two years of hard work and no pay, I closed the doors of my digital marketing agency and applied for a job.

At that moment, I was very happy that somebody hired me.

Two years later I decided to leave that job to launch a new agency.

Within a year, we were making a nice living.

Six years later, we're one of the top growth companies in the Inc 5000.

So, what made the difference in my second agency?

In my first agency, every time I landed a new client, I hoped it was the sign I had finally broken through.

Somebody I met at BNI or the Chamber would tell a friend. I'd build their website, pay most of the bills I was late on, get them on a hosting package and then… CRICKETS.

So, I'd try a few things to rank my site higher. I'd publish some articles and I'd make sure I went to twice as many networking meetings the next month.

However, the recurring revenue barely trickled in. I'd get one or two gigs that helped me catch up on bills, and I told myself it would get better.

I had to recognize that it wouldn't change. And I didn't know the way out.

► I didn't have a strategy to grow to the next level.
► I didn't have a roadmap for success.

At that point, I didn't have a choice. So, I applied for jobs.

Two years later, I decided to set up another agency – and this time would be different.

► This time I had a strategy that would work.
► This time I had a roadmap for success.

Fortunately, I was right. I did have a strategy and a roadmap that would make it work this time.

The first time around, I didn't understand the problems I faced in the market. So, I never knew what would work.

Discovering the Roadmap

What I 'm going to share with you in this book is the plan that we started implementing from day one.

This took us straight to a very successful business within a year. And it's pushed us forward to even bigger dreams.

It's a roadmap that we have fine-tuned in our own business and applied it in other agencies over and over. It can do the same for you.

Now I'm not going to BS you, this isn't turnkey or get rich quick.

It does involve some difficult decisions and some hard work.

But it's a roadmap that transformed my life and the lives of many others we've worked with.

Throughout the pages of this book, I will share that roadmap with you and show you how you too can experience greater success, freedom, and impact.

Who is Josh Nelson and why should I read this book?

My name is Josh Nelson. I'm going to teach you how to land clients, deliver amazing systematized results, retain your clients at the highest level possible, and scale your business. This book, The Seven Figure Agency Roadmap, reveals the key strategies that drive a million-dollar digital marketing agency.

There are plenty of agencies out there in the startup phase of their business. Maybe they earn up to $5,000 per month at first, and they're barely making a living. I call that survival. They will always peak at a certain level because they're spread too thin, and their marketing is ineffective. They don't have enough leads, appointments, clients or money. My job is to help them launch and double their income quickly. If that's what you need, pay close attention; this book will be very helpful for you.

The second thing I do (which occupies about 90% of my time) is to help agencies scale their business. This group, part of my Seven Figure Agency Mastermind, Mentorship & Mastery program is already earning $15,000 a month or more. My job is to help them scale their business and give them three things:

► More Money
► More Meaning (They are helping their clients and building a team)
► More Freedom

I help them build a business that is the basis for a wonderful, liberated, and full life.

I don't know where you are right now in your agency. I'd love to know what you need most. Do you need to launch because you're not at $15,000 per month yet? Or do you need to scale?

Josh Nelson

WORKBOOK

► My goal here is to create the world's best book for agencies on how to grow and scale their business. This book is packed full of strategies and tools I used to take my agency to well over $1 million per year and make the Inc 5000 list of fastest-growing companies the past four years in a row— the same strategies, tools and worksheets I use with clients in my Mastermind, Mentorship & Mastery program.

► You can download them all from www.SevenFigureAgency.com/kit. Jump on the link, download the kit, and get ready to get busy.

► Keep your worksheets handy and complete them as you read the book.

INTRODUCTION

This book is your roadmap to breaking $1 million in your digital marketing agency over the next 12 months.

I know that sounds like a bold statement, especially perhaps for some of you that have been at this game for years and years. And you're like, "How would I ever get to a million in 12 months?"

Well, the fact is, if you just do the math, $83,000 per month makes you a seven figure agency.

BOTTOM LINE: If you could land 5 new clients per month at $1,350+ monthly then you can build 7 Figure Agency in just 12 months...

If you can land five new clients per month at $1,350 per month, that would put you on a run rate to beat Seven Figures.

So, that's what this book is all about. I'm going to be sharing real examples of other digital marketing agencies that have gone to Seven Figures.

We're going to unpack the model; we're going to help you build a plan and set yourself up for tremendous success.

Facing the 3 Big Challenges

Let's start with the reality that growing a digital marketing agency and trying to build something of significance comes with many challenges.

There are three major ones that I hear about from all the digital marketing agencies I talk with. And, when I share more of my story with you in a moment, you'll see that I've faced all of them myself.

1. The digital agency market is overrun

There are hundreds of digital marketing agencies in every city across the United States.

There are major companies like ReachLocal, Scorpion, Hibu & many others, that have millions and millions of dollars to invest.

And then pretty much anybody with a laptop and a computer can call himself or herself an internet marketing consultant or agency. So, your prospects are getting bombarded from every angle.

2. Traditional methods of attracting clients no longer work

In today's marketplace, it's hard to even get your prospect's attention, especially if you're using the traditional means of cold-calling and cold email.

Every small business owner gets cold-called for digital marketing at least four times a day.

They're getting calls every day, they're getting emails every day, they're getting people showing up at their office.

When it's hard to get your prospect's attention, it follows that it's really hard to land clients on a consistent basis.

But the fact is, if we can't land clients, we don't have a business.

3. It's hard to get results

Then, when we do get clients, it's hard to get them results.

The paradigm is constantly shifting. Is it SEO, is it pay-per-click? Is it Facebook ads? Is it funnels? Is it branding?

So, what do you need to actually do to make sure you get your clients a tangible, measurable result and return on investment?

And how can you do it in a way that takes the pressure off you to do everything yourself?

Without the right system and the right team, all of that becomes very difficult.

Finding the Right Model

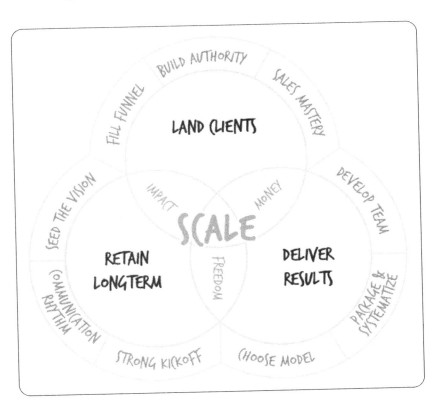

Against that background, it can often feel like trying to build a successful agency means we're taking one step forward and one step back. Like we're on a hamster wheel. We can maybe get a client, but then we lose the client.

Because if we can't get them results, they're not going to stay with us long-term and if we can't retain, then we don't have a business.

So, we need to figure out a way to do these three things…

► Land clients consistently
► Serve them to get them great results
► Retain them long-term

That's what we all want. We don't want to just get clients; we want to serve them well. We want them to get a great return on investment.

You need the right model to do that.

It needs to be able to deliver consistent growth and momentum to enable you to build the agency that serves your desired lifestyle and that will help you serve your family while growing your business to the next level.

That's the model that I'm going to outline to you in this book.

But first, let me share part of my backstory so you know how I got here.

My Story

Today I run a seven-figure digital marketing agency. We've got a team of 30 full-time employees and we made the Inc. 5000 list of fastest-growing companies in the United States the last four years in a row.

But I will say that wasn't always my experience. It wasn't like I just magically got to multiple seven figures.

I started my first agency back in 2004, it was called Develacom, and it was just a web design and hosting company.

I ran it for the better part of four years. And it failed miserably.

I had the wrong model. I was selling websites for a $1,000 to $1,500 in a one-time fee and then $50 per month of recurring revenue.

After four years of running this business and trying my best to get it off the ground, and just not getting where I needed it to be, I had to shut it down.

And it was a very painful experience because I borrowed $10,000 from my dad.

I come from a missionary family. I've got three older sisters and I spent the first 10 years of my life in Haiti.

So, if you can imagine a missionary with a $24,000 a year income, borrowing $10,000 from him was like borrowing $100,000.

But he did it. I don't know where he got it. He might have taken out a second loan or something, but he gave me the $10,000.

That meant a lot to me and I really, really, really needed this to work.

So, I took that money, and I tried to run the business. I was working 60 to 80 hours every single week, but only making enough money to cover the cost of running a business.

Since I was selling websites, it would be $1,000 a site. Even if I sold six clients in a month—and I could do that on a pretty consistent basis—I would spend all of that just to cover my business expenses, not even my living expenses.

I was working 60 to 80 hours every single week, but only making enough money to cover the cost of running a business.

Month after month, year after year, I was working 14 to 16 hours a day, chasing down clients. I was doing all of the standard things, like sitting in BNI meetings, making cold calls, sending out fliers to just about anybody I could, being a very generalist agency with that model.

Then, after years of paying myself nothing, not having any momentum or anything to show for it, I wound up shutting the business down.

It really was one of the hardest things I ever had to do, to go to my dad, who had believed in me and invested this $10,000 and tell him, "I'm sorry, this just didn't work. I've got to go and get a real job now."

So, I left and went into corporate America for a little bit.

I worked at a couple of big companies like ADP and Data Impact. I learned how to sell, but I didn't enjoy it. I wasn't passionate about it. I wanted to run an agency, and I wanted to serve local businesses.

I was always a big student of the game and I was reading books like Robert Kiyosaki's Rich Dad, Poor Dad and T. Harv Eker's Secrets of the Millionaire Mind.

If you haven't read those books, I highly recommend them. In his book, Secrets of the Millionaire Mind, Eker says, "To become a millionaire, to really have a millionaire mind, you have to run your own business."

But he adds, and this stood out to me, "You don't necessarily have to go and start your own business and do it yourself. You can work for somebody that runs the type of business you want to run and get in the corridor."

I realized, "Hey, that's not a bad idea. I can get paid to learn how to run this business and pick up some useful knowledge."

So, I landed a job with ReachLocal, one of the big pay-per-click management companies. They're currently doing $700 million a year in revenue.

The Turning Point

I worked there for about two years. I was one of their top sales guys and I learned a lot.

I learned what the right model was. Don't worry, I'm going to go into more detail, but to summarize, it's about prioritizing recurring revenue and making sure that the monthly fee is large enough that the numbers start to scale.

And, most importantly, I found a belief that I never had before. That belief was that local businesses will gladly pay between $1,000 and $5,000 a month for internet marketing services. Especially if they think there's going to be a tangible return on investment.

I truly lacked this belief early in my business. That's why I was selling a one-time fee, and that's why, in my mind, $250 a month was the most anybody would ever pay for these types of services, but at ReachLocal, I discovered the truth.

However, something that frustrated me was how ReachLocal wasn't generating great results for our clients. They were spending the money, but I didn't think they were spending it wisely. The clients simply weren't getting a great return on their investment.

They were spending the money, but I didn't think they weren't spending it wisely.

As a sales rep at ReachLocal, your job consists mainly of selling the client (through any means necessary). It's a lot of cold calling and sitting and networking in meetings. Then, you've got to go and meet with that client in person and review the call reports.

I was building a relationship with my clients. I was sitting in BNI meetings and I was getting to know these people and I had to go out and meet with them in person and look at the reports with them.

I'd have them look me dead in the eyes and say, "There's no return on investment here." And that was extremely painful.

At that point, I felt I knew what the right model was. I knew that I could sell it. And I had seen thousands of other sales reps selling those services on literally a weekly basis throughout the country. I felt ready to start my own company.

And so, I started my current agency, Plumbing & HVAC SEO, in 2011. We grew it to seven-figures in just under two years serving a very specific niche – Plumbing & HVAC Contractors. Currently, we're running $370,000 a month in recurring revenue and made the Inc 5000 list of fastest-growing companies in the US the last 4 years in a row.

I don't say any of this to brag, but instead to impress upon you that what I'm going to be sharing here isn't from a book that I read. It's not just some theory that I think might be a good way to grow a digital marketing agency.

I've done it, and I've lived it. I've shared it with other people that have had similar results.

And now I'm excited to share it with you.

Sharing the Success

I'm excited to unpack the model for you as we go through this book because I know the impact it can have.

I've shared my backstory and how I've achieved my success. Now I want to talk about something more important than that, and that's how over the last three or four years, I've also taken what I have learned, and I've shown other digital marketing agencies how to do the same.

At this point, I've worked with at least 100 digital marketing agency owners and I've been able to help guys like:

► Allan Hillsburg, who decided he was going to focus on funeral homes and is now a seven figure digital marketing agency owner.

► Jeff Fisher, who went from a pretty stagnant start to being able to position himself within his niche and sold it last year. He now works with us as a success coach.

► Brian Stearman, who started focusing on lawn care maintenance companies and in just 12 months has built a seven figure agency and is continuing to grow at a rapid pace.

► And many others

You can put stock in what I'm going to be sharing with you because I have done it and am currently doing it, and I've helped others do the same.

I applaud you for taking time out to think about your plan, to invest in yourself, and to figure out what it is you need to do to get things going.

Closing the Gap

My commitment to you is that I'm going to share a plan that, if followed, will help you accelerate your agency to $1 million in annual revenue over the next 12 months.

I know that's bold. So, let's take a step back.

I want you to think about what your current monthly recurring revenue is.

1. Write down your current monthly recurring revenue:

_____

Now I want you to think about where you want to be. If we could project forward to next year, where would you like to be from a revenue perspective? Do you want to be at $30,000 by the end of the 12 months, or do you want to be at $83,000 putting you at seven figures? Where do you truly want to be?

2. Write down your desired monthly recurring revenue 12 months from now:

_____

Now I want you to think about the gap. This is the truly important number. To identify the gap, subtract your current monthly recurring revenue from your desired monthly recurring revenue.

Desired Monthly Recurring Revenue _____

LESS Current Monthly Recurring Revenue _____

= Gap _____

I want you to spend a couple of minutes thinking about these numbers. Because the clearer you can get on the numbers, and especially the gap, the more you can make it tangible and real. Thinking like this will enable you to be able to put together a plan to get the work done and make your desired goal a reality.

What I'm going to share with you here is the fastest way to close that gap from wherever you're at today to where you want to go.

The model I'm going to share with you here is how we grew from zero to seven figures and have continued to grow to multiple seven figures. And it is the same model we have used to help more than 100 other agency owners follow a similar path.

So, if you pay close attention, I can help you to close that gap quickly and effectively.

SEVEN FIGURE FUNDAMENTALS

In this chapter, we'll look at some of the fundamentals that are key to achieving your success in building a seven figure agency.

We'll then go on to cover the detailed steps you need to take to make it happen.

Here are the main elements:

- ► The 5 Stages from Start Up to Significance
- ► Aiming for 7 Figures
- ► Deciding Your Destination
- ► Following the Rule of Five Ones
- ► Developing Your 7 Figure Plan

Let's go through each individually.

The 5 Stages from Start Up to Significance

I find within digital marketing agencies, you're in one of five stages in your business.

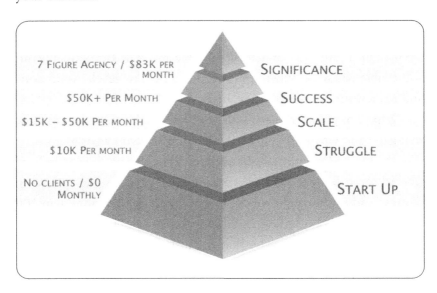

▶ **Start Up:** The first stage is Start-Up. That means you don't really have any clients. That's exciting because you have a feeling of new opportunity and are eager to go out and seize the day.

But it's also a highly stressful time because there's no money coming in.

At Start-Up phase, it's all on you. You must land the clients, serve the clients, do the marketing, do the positioning, and do the work to get the clients coming to you.

If you're in Start-Up phase making less than $10,000 per month for any period, anywhere from three to nine months, soon, you're broke.

So, ideally, nobody wants to stay in Start-Up for long. You want to move past that stage as quickly as possible.

▶ **Struggle:** The next stage is Struggle. This is where you're making $10,000 to $15,000 a month in recurring revenue and you probably have 10 or 15 clients.

That's a struggle because there's not quite enough money to pay your bills, never mind hire anybody to help you out.

What's frustrating with Struggle is that you've got some clients, you finally have work to do but it's still completely on you. There's not quite enough money to build a team.

▶ **Scale:** A key change happens once you break the $15,000 a month barrier. You go to a phase called Scale.

There are lots of new challenges in the Scaling phase but it's really when opportunities start to open up for you.

When you've got $15,000 a month in recurring revenue, you have enough money to at least cover your base needs, and you can start to invest back into the business.

You can invest in processes, people, and in the things that are going to move you to the next level.

It starts to get exciting when you're in that Scale phase because that's where you start to have enough financial resources to systematize your marketing and your fulfillment a little bit so you're not doing everything yourself.

I would like to see you at a minimum of $15,000 over the next six to nine months getting to the Scale phase, where you are between $15,000 and $50,000 per month.

But ultimately, the next phase, Success, which is $50,000+ and Significance, which is achieving a seven figure agency—is really where your life completely changes.

► **Success:** The Success level is when you're making at least $50,000 per month in recurring revenue.

Again, you have a lot more opportunity at that point to build your team and make it so you're not doing everything yourself.

► **Significance:** The ultimate destination is seven figures, Significance. To reach seven figures, you need to be making a minimum of $83,000 a month in recurring revenue.

My goal in this book is to show you how to reach this level in a comfortable way. We'll talk more about that in a moment.

SEVEN FIGURE ACTION

Take a moment to write down where you are now on this scale, where you want to be in 12 months' time, and where you want to be in three years' time.

Now _____

12 months _____

3 years _____

Aiming for Seven Figures

The reason I called my training organization "Seven Figure Agency," is because it's my mission to help as many agency owners as possible get to seven figures and beyond.

I really believe something magical happens in your life and in your business when you can get to seven figures.

Maybe you've set a goal for yourself to get there in a few months or in a few years or perhaps not at all yet.

But I want to talk about why reaching seven figures is important.

The big reason why I believe it's important to aim for a seven figure agency is that I really believe that seven figures is where your life truly changes:

► You earn more money
► You have more freedom with your time
► You make more impact

We'll now look at each of these elements.

More Money

One of the reasons I got into business was because I wanted to have the financial resources to live my desired lifestyle. I wanted to be able to serve my family.

Just beyond the seven figure mark is where my life really changed, and I was able to take care of my family in a way that I never had before.

I've got a beautiful wife, Yesenia, and we've got two kids – Brandon and Ryan, and my world revolves around them. It revolves around providing for them, spending time with them, and giving them good experiences.

That's a key reason I want to be successful in my business. Getting to Significance gave me the ability to buy my dream house in Miami, to drive luxury cars, to put the kids in the best schools and to travel how and when we want.

Also, as I mentioned previously, my dad is a missionary and I want to be able to support spiritual endeavors, as well. (And yes, I did get to pay my dad back, which was huge).

More Freedom

However, one of the most significant results of my business currently isn't just the money. It's the freedom to make choices about how I spend my time.

At seven figures, you can have the freedom to not have to do it all yourself. You are getting enough revenue to put a team in place to help with fulfillment, prospecting, client management and everything else that once fell on just your shoulders.

I've got a team, and I've got systems in place. And because of this, I'm able to go two or three weeks at a time on family vacations. For example, I just got back from a week in Orlando, and my family and I take a couple of cruises every single year.

More Impact

Another key benefit at that level is you know that you're making an impact. You can see that your clients are staying with you because they're getting a return on their investment and you're able to pour into the lives of the people that you employ.

I really want to impress upon you that this is not just about making some more money. It's not just about having more clients. It's also about giving yourself the opportunity to serve others and to live your desired lifestyle, whatever that means for you.

For different people, that means different things, such as:

- ► Ministry
- ► Family
- ► Impact on others
- ► Ferraris and Lamborghinis
- ► Partying
- ► Luxury Travel

Whatever it means to you, that's what we want to help you achieve. We want to help you build to that seven figure level so that you can live that lifestyle and build a legacy.

That's what my Seven Figure Agency Growth Plan is about.

My goal with this is to move at least 100 digital marketing agencies to seven figures or Significance, because I know the life change that can create.

 SEVEN FIGURE ACTION

Take a moment now to think about why growing your digital marketing agency as aggressively as possible is important for you. Is it one of the things I have mentioned above, or do you have your own dreams?

Write it here: _____

_____

_____

_____

_____

Deciding Your Destination

One of the most important foundations of your Seven Figure Agency Growth Plan is clarity of goals.

Without goals, you're almost like a sailboat out at sea where there's no wind. You're just sitting there stagnant.

I'm a big fan of Brian Tracy, he's got some great training about goals and self-development. A quote I love from his book, *Goals! How to Get Everything You Want Faster Than You Ever Thought Possible* is, "Success is goals, all else is commentary."

What that means to me is that you can have lots of different things going on in your life, things that bog you down, or things that keep you busy. But if you don't have clarity about your goals for what you're going to accomplish in the next 12, 24, 36 months, then you're stuck in the commentary. You're being kept busy with nonsense.

Any time I have a slowdown in my life, a slowdown in my progress, it's important for me to realize that I've lost track of my goals and where I really want to go in a specific amount of time.

So, I want you to spend a little time mapping out some goals.

I believe that, without goals, you're almost like a sailboat out at sea where there is no wind. You're just sitting there stagnant. There's no momentum to carry you forward.

But when you do take the time to write down clear goals and put some mechanisms in place to hold yourself accountable, it's almost like you can create your own wind. You can create your momentum and start to accelerate into the direction that you want to go in.

So, what I want to do is just re-convince you of the importance of having goals and the importance of writing those goals down and building that plan.

The goal framework that's worked great for me and that I'm going to encourage you to embrace is to have your goals written down with a plan. As well as longer-term goals, you also have short-term goals that are more tangible so that you can wrap your head around them.

You should have:

► Monthly goals
► Quarterly goals
► One-year goals

So, you are setting out what you're going to get done on a monthly, quarterly and annual basis.

Then, most importantly, you should make sure that you have a stopping point, so that:

► At the end of the month, you're going to stop, and you're going to reflect
► At the end of the quarter, you're going to stop, and you're going to reflect
► At the end of the year, you're going to stop, and you're going to reflect

This was a gamechanger for me because I would always set goals and I'd even write them down in a workbook. But then it would just kind of be sent into the ether, and there were no teeth to it.

I realized that you need to structure your world, your life, and your business around setting a goal. Then take the time to pause and ask yourself if you accomplished the goal. If you did, celebrate that. If you didn't, reflect on what you did wrong, what you could have done differently, or what action you may have failed to take.

When you start to do that, you can develop one of the most important muscles that there is, in my opinion, which is the ability to set an intention, do the activity, and accomplish the desired outcome.

This was a gamechanger for me, and it was a gamechanger for my business partner, Dean. And it is what enabled us to move forward.

Which is why I want to encourage you to follow this mechanism.

What I want for you is to have a clear plan that's built to win that can give you the consistent growth, which ultimately gives you the ability to build a truly successful agency and live your desired lifestyle.

🔊 SEVEN FIGURE ACTION

Take a moment to write down one big goal in each category.

Monthly Goals: _____

Quarterly Goals: _____

One-year Goals: _____

Following the Rule of Five Ones

One of the big breakthroughs for me in developing my Seven Figure Agency and accelerating our growth was when I learned about something called the "Rule of Five Ones."

I initially learned this through Taki Moore of "Million Dollar Coach." But he got it from Clay Collins, the owner and founder of Lead Pages. He was researching businesses that grow super-fast to multiple seven figures and identifying what made them work so well. It boiled down to the fact that they have a very simplified business model.

So, if you too want to grow super-fast to seven figures, I encourage you to really focus on simplifying what you do.

This is a theme that will come up in more detail in other parts of the book but let me just unpack what the Rule of Five Ones is in relation to a seven figure agency.

▶ One target market. In my agency, we serve plumbing and HVAC contractors. That's our market. When I moved from being a generalist to a specialist in one market, everything accelerated.

▶ One lead generation strategy. While there are many ways to get clients, the fastest way to succeed is having one very good lead generation strategy that you do on a consistent basis.

▶ One conversion mechanism. There are lots of ways you can sell the client, such as webinars, live events and one-on-one selling. You want to become great at one and focus on that.

▶ One program. You should offer one core program to your clients that can deliver the results they are looking for. It should not be a la carte, for example: a website here, web hosting there, and a custom application over there. You could have variations of the program for certain specific needs, but you should not be custom-building everything you get.

▶ One year. You need to allow enough time to provide good service in each element before you consider adding anything else.

We'll come back to elements of that in more detail as we go through the book, but I want to put it in front of you now.

Case Study: Following The Rule of Five Ones

Alan Hillsberg started his agency back in 2007. He spent years as a generalist serving anyone who needed internet marketing services. He would have defined his market as "any small/medium size business" that needed to generate more leads via the internet. At one point he was working with an attorney, a restaurant, a Med Spa, and an auto shop, but his agency was failing to produce a profit. He was working hard (50+ hours per week, 7 days a week) but not making the money that he needed to support his family.

In search of answers, he sat on one of my training webinars and latched onto this concept of being niche-specific, charging monthly recurring revenue & aggressively going after clients in the niche. After a lot of thought & deliberation, he landed on funeral homes as his niche and started his new division called "Funeral Home Marketing Services". This changed everything for him in his business. He now had a clear target, strong message & a great systematized program to offer what was uniquely suited for that space (with a monthly recurring fee starting at $997). Over the next 3 years, he proceeded to grow his agency to over $90,000 a month in recurring revenue and gaining 5-7 new clients a month consistently. He now runs a 7 figure digital marketing agency that makes a great profit, and he has the financial freedom to live his desired lifestyle.

You can listen to a full interview with Alan Hillsberg on how he built and grew his agency by going to

https://www.sevenfigureagency.com/alan

Developing Your 7 Figure Agency Growth Plan

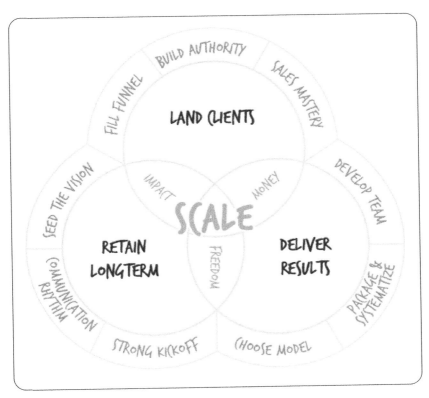

Now, let's talk about the Seven Figure Agency Growth Plan. What I want for you more than anything else is a business that can scale. Something that will provide:

► Money for you and your family. I want you to be able to afford to take adventures, to buy the things that you want, and to support the community.

► Freedom from having to do it all yourself. A scaled business gives you freedom because you have a team that handles the work and handles the client relationships and handles everything else.

Sure, it's possible to build a seven figure agency and do it all yourself, but you're more bound to the business than when you didn't have anything going. I don't want that. I want you to have freedom.

► Impact and knowing that what you do matters. It's important that you're serving your team that you're investing in to do the work. And that you're serving your clients and that they're getting great results.

I really feel that's what we want to build, and that's what the Seven Figure Agency Growth Plan is about.

The key to the plan is that Every Digital Marketing Agency is built on three pillars of success:

► Land clients
► Deliver results for clients
► Retain clients long-term

Let's drill into these in more detail.

Land Clients

This is how we generate leads, online and off, and how we get them to come to us pre-positioned to buy at premium rates and then hire us for our services.

► In order to land clients on a consistent basis, you must be able to fill your funnel—get prospects coming to you, ready to buy. You must be able to get people coming in who trust you— people who raised their hand, who have expressed interest, and who ultimately at the bottom of the funnel become clients.

► You must build your authority and position yourself as the expert so you're not having to chase people down. If you're seen as the authority and they believe you're an expert in their type of business and you've got a proven model, they're willing to pay premium rates. There's very little sales resistance, and you have consistency and flow.

► You need to have sales mastery. You have to know how, when people do raise their hand, you can have a great business conversation, you can tap into their needs and their desires, and you can make it clear what it is that you have and what you can bring to the table.

That's what we will talk about in the first part of this book.

Deliver Results

This is how we package our service offering in a way that gets consistent, measurable results and a tangible return on investment.

The key is to do it in a way that frees you up from doing custom work for each client and having to do it all yourself.

► You've got to choose a model that serves you. I talked earlier about the model that I was running for years when my business went under, and I had to shut it down. But you need a model that's going to serve you, and I'll talk about that.

► You need to package and systematize. That means you must package it in a way that gets the client results. Package it with the knowledge that you are going to do something specific and the client is going to get a specific result. Then you need to systematize it in a way that means you don't have to do it all yourself. Do this so that you have everything mapped out and know it's going to get done well without being reliant on you.

► Eventually, you scale to a certain level where you can develop a team so that servicing the needs of the clients takes care of itself, the fulfillment of the work takes care of itself and the account management and ongoing retention of the client takes care of itself.

In the second segment of the book, I'll show you what I've learned about serving your clients well, systematizing your offering and building a winning team.

Retain Long-term

This is how we keep those clients with us month-after-month. If you can't retain, then you can't grow, and you will be taking two steps forward and one step back.

► To retain, you must make sure you've engineered a strong kickoff process.

That means you've got a great onboard experience. There are certain experiential things right out of the gates where they can feel they made a great decision and they chose the right company. They will feel like you are trustworthy and will get the job done.

► You must have a good communication rhythm to retain clients. It's not as simple as sending them an automatic report.

You need to engineer what you're going to do every month and how you're going to communicate. What reports are you giving them? What is your team doing on those monthly calls so that they feel like you are working with them to accomplish their goals? You need to have a good synergy happening here.

► You also need to seed the vision so they see why they should stay with you not just one month or five months, but they stay with you for years and years.

One thing I found that will make them leave quicker than anything else is perceived indifference and the sense that you have taken them as far as they're going to go. So, you must constantly be helping them see what's next.

For example, if your program is setting up a website and doing SEO and pay-per-click, once that's up and running and they're getting some calls, you can come across like you've done your job.

If they don't feel like you're looking at the next thing, whatever that is: chat bots or some new Facebook advertising strategy or some new content thing—if you're not constantly seeding the vision of what's next that you're going to bring to the table, you're going to have massive churn.

In part three of the book, we'll unpack some of the best strategies and techniques for keeping clients onboard as long as possible.

The Seven Figure Agency Model

That's the Seven Figure Agency Model:

Land Clients. Deliver Results. Retain Long-term.

If you can get the three elements within each of these really honed in, you'll have a business that grows, scales and expands.

You can do OK winging it. But hitting a million dollars – at least for me – took some serious focus on these three core areas in my agency.

Once you get all of this fleshed out, and you get to a level of mastery, getting to seven figures and having a business that truly serves you in that way becomes very natural.

That's what we'll do in the remaining chapters of this book.

How to Read this Book

I suggest that you read the whole book first quickly to get an overview and an understanding.

You'll probably find that some parts are more urgent than others, depending on where you are right now.

Then, as you work through the book for the second time, here is where you take time to follow the Seven Figure Agency Growth Plan actions as you reach each appropriate stage.

The main thing you need to do from the outset is to make sure you choose the right model to build your business on. For that reason,

I recommend that you start working on the section on choosing a model first.

The reason I suggest starting with the model is because, if you're not clear on what you're going to sell and what you're going to charge and what your business model's going to look like, there's no sense figuring out how you're going to market or how you're going to position yourself. You'd just be running on a hamster wheel to nowhere.

Once you have that right, you can fill your funnel so that you have leads coming in on a consistent basis. Then you'll be ready to change your systems to deliver the right results and to ensure you keep clients for the long-term.

Those are the fundamentals. So, let's get started. I'm excited to share this journey to seven figures with you!

PART ONE

LAND CLIENTS

1

LAND CLIENTS 1: FILL FUNNEL

Creating a Massive Surge of Ideal
Clients to Fuel Your Agency Growth

The first key to success with your digital agency is having a steady stream of high-quality leads coming to you on a consistent basis.

The challenge of this is that it's almost impossible to get the attention of prospective clients. But more than that, oftentimes how we get their attention will dictate how the sales relationship goes.

Oftentimes how we get the attention of potential clients will dictate how the sales relationship goes.

So, if we only had one method for landing clients—the one that almost everybody teaches, which is: cold calling, cold drop-ins, sitting in network meetings—oftentimes once you do get their attention, you have a hard sell.

That happens because the way that you arrived at their door was forced or they didn't really see you as the expert. They didn't see you as the guy that understands their space. You will have to work hard to convince them that you can help them.

Have you ever experienced a time where you really have had to hard sell people? It is a lot of hard work convincing them that you are the person who will get them the results they are looking for.

Because of that, we wind up with an empty calendar.

It sucks to chase people down and it sucks to do hard sells.

So, either we don't get enough appointments, or we avoid doing the activity that generates those appointments. And if we don't have a full calendar of appointments or we're busy selling people what we can do or how we can help them, we don't generate the revenue.

We wind up in this place where we've got to close the business, we've got to go back and get a regular J-O-B.

The alternative is to get prospects raising their hands, having already been influenced by you and having some understanding of what your value is.

Now, instead of you having to chase them down, they are saying, "Yes, I'd be interested in seeing what you have to say."

That's the secret to getting plenty of appointments and consistent deal flow.

You've got to get out of the habit of one deal a quarter or one deal every now and then. Instead, you want to move to consistently landing clients on a monthly basis.

When you do that, that's when you are starting to build a seven figure agency.

Methods of Filling the Funnel

The first thing you need to work out is how you're going to get clients into the fold on a monthly basis.

Then you can figure out the other stuff in terms of fulfillment and in terms of retention.

When it comes to landing clients on a consistent basis, there are a lot of different avenues and a lot of different things you can do.

However, it really breaks down to the following five categories:

1. Cold Outreach
2. Marketed Lead Generation
3. Inbound Marketing
4. Associations / Speaking
5. Joint Ventures

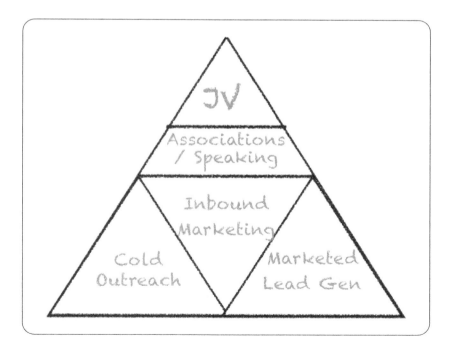

I believe there's a place for all of these. We get business through pretty much all of these avenues. But certain ones work better than others and certain ones are quicker than others.

All these methods can have an impact and you want to find one that you're really good at, and then spend most of your energy on it. Let's look at them more closely.

1. Cold Outreach

The one we usually hear about is just straight up Cold Outreach. There's a way to do it where you get people to raise their hand so it's not totally cold, but they at least give you a soft raised hand.

There's just doing cold calls, sending cold emails, doing brute force to shake the bushes and get clients to come in. We'll talk about this in a lot more detail in a moment.

2. Marketed Lead Generation

Marketed Lead Generation is running Facebook ads, pay-per-click campaigns, doing direct mail, doing things to go out and really market to your database or niche and get clients.

The beauty of Marketed Lead Generation is that you can control your destiny.

While you can also have some control over your destiny with cold outreach, with marketed leads, if you have the financial resources to invest, which some do and some don't, you can generate enough leads to fill the calendar through that one mechanism alone.

3. Inbound Marketing

I'm a huge fan of Inbound Marketing. There's a great book called, Inbound Marketing, by the guys who make HubSpot. It's an amazing book, which you should read.

With Inbound Marketing, it's just your energy that goes into getting the clients in this way.

- ► It's you putting out good content, putting on webinars, conducting interviews, and putting information out on blogs.
- ► It's you putting stuff out into cyberspace, getting people to be influenced by your expert status, and then come to you.
- ► It's putting out information into the world that your prospects would find and think, "Man, that's good. That person must know what they're talking about."

We're going to spend a lot of time on Inbound Marketing and how you can get clients coming to you already positioned to buy.

This is magnetically attracting people, which is one of my main plays and one of my favorite strategies for landing clients.

---

4. Associations and Speaking

Within any niche, there are associations – there are national associations, local associations, associations within associations.

I've found this is a great shortcut because if you can get into the association, you get access to their list. You get affiliation where you can call and say, "We're national members of the Plumbing and HVAC PHCC and we just wanted to send you some information. We wanted to invite you to this webinar." It helps shortcut the process.

This is one of the most powerful plays that you can tap into to get clients.

Also, associations gather. They get together at local events and national events, and you can get in front of your ideal prospects where they are hanging out.

So, in place of the need to cold call and interrupt them, you can get them where they're already hanging out.

The most powerful play within associations is speaking. If you're the person at the front of the room educating your prospects on the best way to land clients or the best way to internet market themselves, your resistance drops to nothing.

They are automatically thinking, "The association put this guy up there. He knows what he's talking about, he's obviously an expert."

That's one of the most powerful ways that you can tap into to get new clients.

Some agencies have used this as their number one breadwinner, and it works extremely well.

5. Joint Ventures (JVs)

Top of the hierarchy is JVs, Joint Ventures. That's just tapping into someone that already sells to your target market.

For example, find somebody who already is a guru within the market or a consultant of some sort within that vertical and you can work out a joint venture.

You may be only one JV away from a Seven Figure business.

They need a reason to introduce you, a reason to let you come speak, a reason to let you do something on their behalf.

You'll find that for some of our most successful members, that's their number one strategy. They found one person that had a massive influence within their type of prospect, and they put together a JV.

In a lot of cases, it's a financial incentive. For example, you might give them 10% of the recurring revenue for each person who signs up as a result of this relationship or something along those lines.

So, you put together a win-win relationship where they're going to promote you, and they're going to make money when you land clients.

We can only go so deep on JVs. Just know that it's a big opportunity, and you should always be looking for it.

JVs are one of those hit or miss things. If you don't have the option of doing one, you must have other strategies that will fill your pipeline and keep you busy.

Always keep an eye on the horizon. Pay attention to who is already selling to your ideal client and try to align yourself with them because it could be a massive gamechanger.

As an example, Jimmy Nicholas has built a great seven figure business, turning over more than $3 million per year. He focuses on orthodontics, and one of his main strategies was to align himself with the number one guru/trainer in the orthodontics space.

He earned that guru's trust, got him to see what he was capable of, and proved himself. Then that guru started introducing Jimmy to their client base.

Through that strategic alliance, that joint venture, his business has blossomed.

Cold Outreach

We're going to focus first on one of the client-landing mechanisms that I've found to work really well that you can control and have good results with, and that's Cold Outreach.

We all must be doing Cold Outreach at some level to build our list and to get prospects to raise their hand.

It's a lever you can control, so we're going to go pretty deep into this topic.

Then in the next segment, we're going to talk about Inbound Marketing which is how to position yourself as the expert. We'll cover very specific things you can do on a weekly and monthly basis to make yourself the authority within your space and get clients coming to you on a consistent basis.

When we look at Cold Outreach, there are four key elements we need to address:

Create Your Foundation Funnel

Build Your List

Run an Outreach Campaign

Nurture Your List

1. The Ultimate Agency Funnel

Before you can really go out and start actively signing up clients, you need to create a foundational funnel that people can enter your world through.

The key elements of this are:

► Clear Target/Niche

► Opt-in incentive

► Appointment

► Hot Lead Follow Up

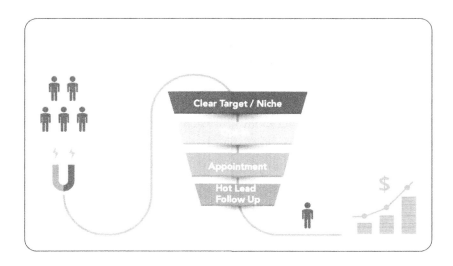

▶ **Clear Target:** First, you need a clear definition of your core niche or market.

We will be looking at that more closely later.

▶ **Opt-in:** Then you need a Lead Magnet of some sort that people can opt-in for.

Whether it's a cheat sheet, a guide, a printed book or a case study, you need something that they can opt-in to in order to enter your world as an email opt-in.

You need something that you can offer to them that makes them see value in the content and causes them to raise their hand to opt-in to your world.

What I've found is that the cheat sheet works best, so you just have something very simple like "The Ultimate Plumbing and HVAC Online Marketing Cheat Sheet" or "The Ultimate Dental Marketing Cheat Sheet.

It just needs to list out the main things they need to know.

The reason it works well is that it's high desire, and it's low commitment.

You can create a good cheat sheet without having to invest a ton of time.

Having that on your website as the main option with a low barrier to entry option is a great play.

As an alternative to a basic cheat sheet, you could offer an internet marketing guide or your keyword list. There are lots of cool things you can offer to your industry that would be interesting.

► **Appointment:** Next, you need an appointment funnel where it's easy for them to go from raising their hand to getting onto your schedule.

Once they opt-in by giving you their e-mail, give them the opportunity to get to your calendar where they can schedule themselves for that type of appointment.

What you want to do is move them from whatever you promote on your website to getting them straight to the appointment funnel, where they can be exposed to you, by opting-in.

Your message should be focused on getting them from interested to actively participating. You do this in the form of scheduling an appointment to talk more one on one.

They didn't just download the cheat sheet because they want the information. They want the result, and the result is best if they have somebody that can implement it for them.

So, what you want to do is offer them the opportunity to sit down, one-on-one, so you two can talk about their business and how you can execute this for them.

You can have lots of different funnels, but you should have one opt-in funnel and one appointment funnel. With this approach, they opt-in and they get the opportunity to sit down with you one-on-one and the ability to choose a time on your schedule.

You can use HighLevel, Calendly, Appointment Core, or anything you find useful. There are lots of different ways to set it up, but that's what you need to have in place.

▶ **Hot Lead Follow-up:** Once you have the lead, it's important that you have an effective follow-up process.

First, you want to have a great follow-up package which can go out after the appointment. I know that when you do that consistently, you can start to close deals consistently.

Then you need to have a tight sales process. Ask yourself, how do you take someone from interested to sold and then what are the steps in between? What is it that they get via email? What specific tasks happen?

This is called a hot lead follow up campaign. It's knowing that, once you have talked to someone, the process is engineered in advance. You know the exact touches the client is going to get to move them from interested to closed.

You want a tight sales process where you can confidently get individuals on the phone, help them understand where there are problems with what they're doing today that is preventing them from getting to where they want to be.

As part of that, you need to give them a solution, "I'm going to do this and I'm going to do that."

We'll talk more about the sales process later.

When you have all that in place, that's where you can start to have a base funnel to build on.

But what often happens when I work with digital marketing agencies is that they have a funnel set up and are creating opportunities to opt-in but they are still struggling because they lack an audience. No one is requesting to opt-in because they aren't reaching their target audience. They don't have their list. Don't worry though, because that is what we will look at next.

2. Build Your List

So how do you get a list? How do you get the names and contact details for the people within your niche, so that you can give them your guide, and so that you can potentially get them on your calendar?

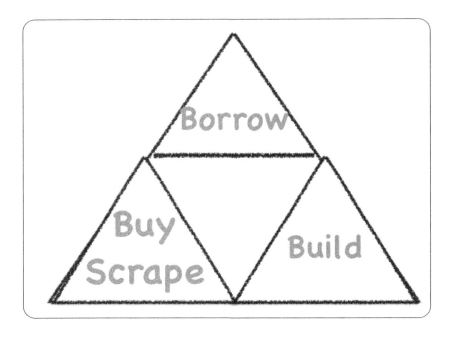

These are the main options for building your list:

► **Buy / Scrape**
► **Borrow**
► **Build**

Buy/Scrape a List

Perhaps the easiest option is to simply buy a list that someone else already has of people in your market. For example, you could buy a list of dentists in South Florida.

There are lots of companies that specialize in selling lists such as SICCode.com, DataAxle (formerly InfoUSA or some other sources) and my favorite ColdLytics.

Another way you can buy a list is from an association. The good thing about an association list is that to become members of the group they had to pay, and you get all their verified details. You also know they are all legitimate people, and you usually get names, addresses, and phone numbers.

Some lists don't include email addresses though, and you might have to employ somebody to go to their websites and identify their emails in case the association doesn't provide it. But this is a great way to get your initial list.

This is one of my favorite ways to get the list within your space because we know that they are pre-vetted. They are known to be buyers because they paid to be part of the association. They probably didn't spend a ton of money, but they still invested to be a part of the association to land on that list.

It's pretty easy to go and join the Plumbing Association or the Damage Restoration Association or the Kindergarten Care Association. With that, you've got a good baseline list of people in your niche.

With an association, you can usually join as a member or as an industry partner. You pay a little bit more to become an industry partner but then your logo goes up on their site. They're effectively saying, "We recommend this company."

You want to get that type of status within the association and then you want to find their events and activities. We'll talk more about that later.

Another way to buy a list is something like Sales Navigator from LinkedIn. A Sales Navigator account costs $79 a month. However, this may give you their private email, not necessarily their business one.

When you buy a list, you can usually specify exactly what you want such as geographic location and business size.

As an alternative to buying a list from someone who already has it, you can "scrape" a list by running a tool such as D7Lead Finder or Lead Kahuna. These tools go out and collects details such as names, phone numbers, email addresses and other contact details of people based on what is posted on the internet. There are a plethora of these types of tools on the market & I've tried just about all of them. While they do provide data there is typically high degrees of inconsistency (wrong industry, out of business, etc). At this point, my best suggestion would be to invest in a paid list (Association, SICCode or ColdLytics) so you are working with solid data. As the saying goes "garbage in, garbage out".

Borrow a List

You also have the option to borrow a list. This is a tremendously powerful play and I'm a big advocate.

Borrowing a list means you find an expert that's already selling to your ideal customer, and you form some type of relationship with them and they agree to mail on your behalf. In some situations, they may even give you their list because there's something to be gained by them by doing so.

Those JV people we talked about and others will already have a list of people in your space.

If you spend a couple of minutes thinking creatively, it's worth the time. Think about who already sells to the fencing contractors that you want to do business with? Who already sells to the people that you want to sell to? Find that JV opportunity and you can get access to their list.

Build a List

Then there's the option to build the list. One way to do this is through inbound marketing.

Your built list is powerful, but it also takes a very long time. We're wanting to get you to seven figures quickly, so we're going to focus on buying and scraping because that's something you can start tomorrow, which will allow you to build your list, and to build your following.

Again, you should be tapping into all your options to build your list, but the ones you have more control over are the buy and scrape options.

You can start right now by following these steps to have a list that you're starting to reach out to proactively.

List Building Tips

Please understand that when you get a list of data, you must constantly be working on that list to make sure it is as accurate and appropriate for your needs as possible.

It's no good having a list of 1,000 people if they don't fit your criteria, like for example, they are in the wrong area or they are the wrong type of business.

If you can get a 1,000 list down to 300 that are in your target market, you will get better results.

Lead Kahuna's a great tool if you're doing cold email outreach but the list you start with may just be a lot of businesses across the country that had the word "carpet cleaning" in their title, for example.

You need to work at this list to make sure it is right for your needs in terms of geography, type of business and size of business.

Marketing guru, Dan Kennedy, says you need to clean your list through at least five steps. You've got to figure out what those five are for your niche.

For example, you might want to know that a carpet cleaning business has a full-time receptionist. If they have a full-time receptionist, that probably means three or four trucks. You can just call them up and ask how many trucks they have; they are not going to ask why you want to know.

One thing I will say is don't try to do this process yourself. You can create a virtual team of people from freelance sites who have the right experience, who know exactly how to do this and have the right tools. You just need to tell them what you want.

There are various steps involved so don't try to get the same person to do all of these things. That's the biggest mistake made.

Get a great researcher. Take your list down to say 400. Then hand that over to a great phone call person. And tell them, "All I want you to do is get an appointment on my calendar for a 15-minute discovery call."

Fiverr has some solid sources for this. I think one of the best is Upwork. You get an infinite supply of people that know how to do certain things. Some people are ninja-like at list building.

I love putting a project out on Upwork and letting people come and say they can build a list for me. You'd be surprised. There are some crazy mechanisms these people can use to shortcut that process.

You can hire someone in the Philippines and they just call someone on the list and ask one or two questions. Pretty soon, your list of 1,000 is narrowed down because you couldn't find emails for 200 of them and 200 didn't have a full-time receptionist.

Ultimately, you end up with a list where you know they're doing more than $1 million, you know they're still in business and you've confirmed they have a full-time receptionist or three trucks or whatever. So, your odds have now gone up dramatically.

You can use a tool like Hunter.io to double-check that the emails on your list are valid and many of the freelancers you can use will have that available.

The advantage of buying a list from InfoUSA, for example, is that it probably starts 80% right, so you're starting with something better.

Protecting Your Domain

If you're doing a lot of cold emails you might want to consider sending from a different email address so that you protect your domain name.

There are lots of ways to handle this. We have a list of like 20,000 plumbing companies. I send well over 100,000 emails every single month at this point. So, I'm not that concerned about it.

However, if you've got a list of like 100 people, or you just added 500, you probably want to protect your main domain. So, you might want to set up something separate.

For example, I suggest, if you're plumberseo.net, get plumberseo.biz. or if you are sevenfigureagency.com, get seven-figure-agency.com.

That way if you get a high spam complaint rate, if you've got issues, you're not blacklisting your core domain. Remember, you want to redirect that new domain to your main website.

3. Run an Outreach Campaign

Once you have your list, then you can start to do some cold outreach to get customers to raise their hands. This way you're not cold calling, but you're getting some people who are pre-dispositioned to hear you out.

We've got a clear target, which is our niche. We've got a solid list of prospects list, and then we must have a mechanism to get their attention.

That mechanism might be cold emails, voice drops, and/or social messenger. I find that if you hit at least three of these four, you can really get their attention.

It's important to note that you must do some volume with cold outreach, you can't just send 10 or 15.

Some of them will raise their hand and tell you that they are interested and want to hear what you have to say. This means you're jumping into conversations with interested people, as opposed to making 100 calls to only get one person who is interested.

There's an important distinction here between using cold outreach to get warm, raised hands versus just cold calling again, and again, and again.

The whole idea is to leverage this so we can get strategy sessions.

Three Campaigns

There are three campaigns for cold outreach that we have found to be extremely effective. These are:

1. One Company in Your Area
2. Can You Handle an Additional "X" This Month?
3. Content Offer

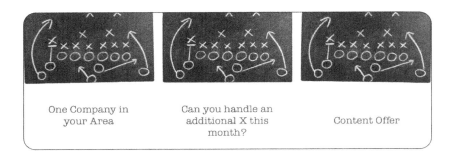

| One Company in your Area | Can you handle an additional X this month? | Content Offer |

Campaign #1: One Company in Your Area

First, is the "One Company in Your Area" campaign. Most of us offer exclusivity, there might only be 325 markets, which means we can serve 325 clients. We know that we're only going to work with one in each market, so we might as well use that to our advantage.

And the fact is, they all want exclusivity. So if you've got it carved out on a city by city basis, you can send an email that's just basically to the effect of, "I'm looking to work with one roofing contractor in the Miami area and I wanted to jump on a quick call with you."

Or you can have a sequence of emails that takes them down the path of, "I'm looking to find one roofing company in Atlanta that I can partner with."

The second message is, "Hey I sent this to you yesterday, did you have a chance to look at it?" Then the next email would be a little bit more detailed, "Just so you know, this is what I've done for other roofers across the country. I'm only going to do it for one in this area. So, it's first come first served."

You put together a multi-step cold outreach campaign using email, web forms and social messenger. You hit them with that same outreach strategy from a lot of different angles.

You'll then get people who reply. "Yeah, I'd be interested in chatting with you about that." That's where you get some raised hands. I've found that this campaign works well.

Having a five or six email and social messenger campaign along those lines is a great way to do cold outreach.

Campaign #2: Can You Handle an Additional "X" this Month?

Another play we're finding that works well is, "Can you handle an additional "X" this month" and sending that out to potential clients.

An example of this is, "Can you handle an additional three to five metal roofing projects this month?"

A lot of people write back, "Yeah, of course, I can. I need more roofing projects."

From those responses, you can follow up and say, "Great. We happen to specialize in helping roofers generate more metal roofing jobs. Let's have a conversation about how we could help."

Ideally, you need to figure out what their high-ticket thing is that they want more of.

For us in plumbing, that's trenchless sewer repair. That job is worth $16,000 or $17,000. So instead of reaching out to all the plumbers and saying, "Could you handle some more plumbing calls?" we reach out and say, "Can you handle an additional two to three trenchless sewer repair projects this month?" Of course, they want more of these.

So, try and figure out the one high-ticket thing and rotate this into your direct outreach.

All you're looking for on that email is the people who respond. And when they do, you jump on them rapidly, "Hey thanks for calling back, I specialize in helping plumbing companies generate more trenchless sewer repair jobs. Let's start a dialog."

Ultimately your goal is to pique their interest in what you can provide for them enough to get them to raise their hand.

Campaign #3: Content Offer

The third play we suggest is a content offer. So, I'm going to talk about lead magnets and putting out great content.

If you've created a cheat sheet or guide, just reach out to them, "I developed this great report on how to generate more leads via the internet for your roofing business, is that something you'd be interested in?" They'll reply back.

You don't send them the guide, you call them up and say, "You requested my guide, I've got it here for you. I just wanted to connect and answer some questions for you. What's the best email?" etc.

That's how you want your cold outreach to come across. It's very text-based, very low-key.

It's not "Click here, do this." That immediately gets ignored.

But if they feel like you wrote them a message and it solicits a response, then that works well.

Consistent Campaigns

To get started, you can take any of these three plays, and you can rotate them.

Start with, "Can you handle an additional two to three jobs?" No response? Then go to, "I'm looking to work with one in your area." No response? Then circle back and drop content on them consistently.

That's how you can get certain people who are ready, and they raise their hand and warm up to wanting to do business. But you also start to plant seeds for long-term business relationships.

All these options work out to be great conversation starters. Ideally, you want to use some version of each of these.

The key insight I want you to take away is to get the list and hit them from multiple angles. Don't expect people to just reply and want to meet with you.

You're still going to have to chase them down because this is still cold outreach, and you want to use all the channels to get their attention.

If you're playing the cold outreach game, this isn't waiting until your ideal client falls into your lap. You've got to be more assertive than you think is rational.

You're going to get certain people who respond, so jump on those. When they do reply, you should call them immediately.

What I mean by that is literally within a couple of minutes of them responding, you need to be on them.

When you call them, they are probably not going to even remember that they replied. So, what I recommend is shooting a Loom video of some sort.

For example, you could do a quick screen recording, "Hey you responded back. You're looking to do an additional three to five trenchless jobs. I wasn't able to get you on the phone, so I wanted to shoot a quick video."

What you do is you pull up their website and you talk about whatever your unique strategy is to get them a result. Then you say, "Let's jump on a call so that we can talk through this."

The point is you just can't send emails and sit on your hands. You've got to call, you've got to create videos, you've got to follow up with Messenger and LinkedIn to break through the noise.

You're not the only person contacting these people. Especially via this mechanism.

The big mistake I see a lot of people make on this front is that they just want to send an email. Well, the fact is, how many emails do you have sitting in your inbox that you've never looked at? A lot. I don't even want to know how many emails I have.

Two backdoor channels that work well are sending a text message if you can get their phone number, and social messenger, either Facebook Messenger and or LinkedIn Messenger.

Do a little bit of extra due diligence beyond just sending an email blast. You can go find that person on LinkedIn and connect with them or find them on Facebook and send a friend request and then send them a message.

If you're a Facebook user, and I'd say most of us are, you get that little pop-up and you pay attention to it. It's a backdoor way to get their attention that most of us aren't tapping into.

After this, of course, we're going to move them to a strategy session. We'll talk more about those later.

The Power of Cold Email

I get questions from people all the time about whether or not sending out cold emails can really have an impact and produce results.

I want to assure you that cold email, with the right structure, with the right list, can be extremely effective.

I sent a cold email to a plumber in Tallahassee and his reply was, "Sure, let's chat. Do you want to send an invite?"

Another big company that we were interested in working with, wrote back, "Steve forwarded me your email, I'm very interested in speaking with you. When can we talk?"

One wrote, "I'm interested. Send me some additional information and costs."

When someone writes back and says, "I'm interested," this is somebody who's very interested. They've got some urgency that I'm tapping into in this situation.

So, yes, cold email can work. It's not my favorite play, but if you get it going consistently and you know that you can systematize it, you can get a virtual assistant to run it for you—once you're big enough.

It's just one channel that's constantly going out, building your database, planting seeds, getting some raised hands, and giving you the ability to land clients consistently.

So, cold outreach should be the entry point for all your prospecting efforts. It can generate two to three great clients every single month if you work it correctly.

Implementation Steps

Here are the three steps that you need to take to turn this into action:

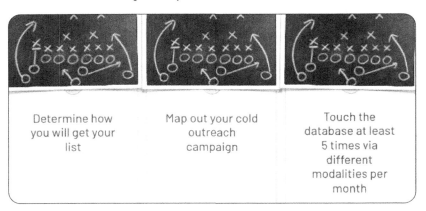

| Determine how you will get your list | Map out your cold outreach campaign | Touch the database at least 5 times via different modalities per month |

Step #1: Determine how you will pull your list

Figure out how you're going to get your list. This means determining where you're going to pull your list from and there are lots of different ways to do this. You can join the association, leverage tools or buy the list from a quality source.

Step #2: Map out your cold outreach campaign

Map out your cold outreach campaign. Which of the three plays will you use? Are you going to take the "One company in your area" or would the, "Hey, I've got this great information to share with you" approach work better for you?

Step #3: Commit to touch the database at least 5 times via different modalities per month

Then you've got to commit to touching the database multiple times through multipe modalities until they say "interested" or "stop". This isn't a scenario where you do a couple of emails here and there.

To get enough volume so that enough people raise their hand, you must send out a lot of messages because the reach has got to be very large.

500 quality touches per month will generate at least five to ten raised hands which can result in one or two clients on a pretty consistent basis. That's been the gamechanger for a lot of our clients and a lot of our members.

When you get 500 messages out every month, 99 percent of them will have no interest, but you are aiming for the one percent.

If they open your communication (email, social message, etc) you want to have enough there to spark their interest and get them to raise their hand. Once they have raised their hand and written back, you know they are interested, and you have them half-way there. The people that reply and show an interest are the ones you want to pursue.

If you're busy all day just cranking on the phone or you're going out and knocking on people's doors, you're not tapping into the potential of volume and so you will have to work so much harder to get the result.

And the result you want in this case is to get strategy sessions.

If you're going to land three to five new clients per month, you must be able to get at least 15 or 20 strategy sessions.

Those are people that have said they are interested, and they let you show them where there's a problem with their current strategy and how you can help.

4. Nurture Your List

So, when trying to land clients, one of our key plays is cold outreach. I just want to make sure I paint the big picture of this. We buy the list, we join associations, and we get names, emails, and contact details.

Then we do direct outreach via cold emails, social messengers, cold calls, voice drops, and through whatever other mechanisms we can to get them to raise their hand.

But the fact is, only a handful of the people will raise their hand. If out of the 500 cold emails you sent out result in 10 or 15 people who raise their hand, that's a pretty good day.

It's a percentage game and it's the lowest percentage game in the business. If all you do is cold outreach, you will not have a great business. It is simply a starting point.

The next step is to nurture that database. You want to nurture them, so they go from, "I got a random email from this person," to, "This person has added value to my life. They have shared valuable resources. They have given me information, the tools I was lacking, and have given me things that can move my business forward."

People call us and they say, "Hey, I've been watching your videos for years. I've been getting your emails for years, and I'm finally ready to hire you guys."

It's no longer about convincing them to hire you, instead, they just need to know if they can. That's really where I want you to go.

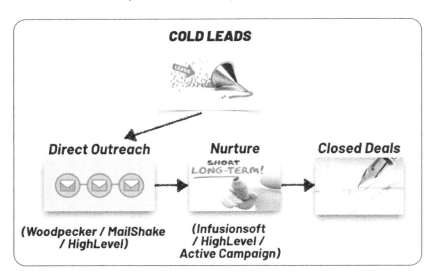

The reason you need to have an aggressive cold outreach strategy is so you can control your destiny.

If you just wait for inbound leads or if you wait for marketed leads, you might be waiting all year and only get a couple of clients.

But, if you get an aggressive outbound strategy where you're sending emails, you're going to get raised hands, you're going to start to develop your list, and you'll be able to control where you're going to end up.

So, you need to nurture that database because those are going to be the clients you want to do business with.

Preparing for the Next Step

This strategy is great for getting the process started and moving in a good direction to some quick wins.

To do that, you want to nurture the ones who raise their hand and get some momentum.

However, ultimately, your ideal client is the one who chose you.

The problem with landing clients only through cold outreach is you're always chasing them down.

Have no doubt about it, you're cold calling them and you're showing up in their inbox unexpected.

Even when they do raise their hand to say they might be interested, if you land a client through cold outreach there's going to be a hard sell involved. And because of this, your close rate is not going to be nearly as high.

I would say a 10% close rate from cold outreach is good because they don't know you. They just got a random message from you, and they have no context to who you are.

Due to these factors, you're going to need a lot more sales appointments to get the same amount of new clients. And ultimately, it's hard to generate sales.

When I was at ReachLocal, chasing clients was the only option. I was cold calling, sitting in network meetings, and chasing people, chasing people, chasing people. There's a place for it but it's got to be baked into what you do.

What you want is prospects that already feel like they know you and they're ready to do business with you.

So, let's dive into that and unpack how we build the authority so that we attract clients who are ready to do business with us.

 SEVEN FIGURE ACTION

Follow the implementation steps outlined on page 96 to:

► Determine how you will pull your list

► Map out your cold outreach campaign

► Commit to touch the database at least 5 times via different modalities per month.

Case Study: Landing Clients With Cold Outreach

Danny Barrera spent his days as an IT analyst for Fox News listening to success story after success story. After hearing an interview with someone who made money doing an e-commerce website and getting his advice, he dove in headfirst. He spent over 10k trying to develop his business, and it failed. But he learned how marketing worked on the internet and learned from his mistakes.

Danny quit his IT job and fully committed himself to the process of starting a digital marketing agency. He started like most of us as a generalist agency taking whoever he could get and quickly realized that was not going to work.

It was tough. Without cashflow, his power was turned off, his car was repossessed, and he ended up getting divorced. He hit the point where he HAD to make this work, or it was all going to be over. During that time, he became great at Search Engine Optimization (SEO), started sales training, and learned how to do cold calling.

He saw one of my old websites, "Contractor SEO", and thought it would be a great idea to model that, but the niche was still too broad & clients were tough to come by. The fact is, 'contractor' could mean so many things (roofer, builder, deck company, pool service, plumber) so his message was not resonating. On a coaching call, he realized that he needed to narrow his niche down even further and decided to focus on "Decorative Concrete Companies" and started his new division called, "Concrete Marketing Crew". He got aggressive with cold outreach and following up via multi-channel as outlined in this chapter and in a matter of 12 months had gone from "broke" to doing over $53K per month in recurring revenue.

You can listen to a full interview with Danny Barrera on how he built and grew his agency by going to

https://www.sevenfigureagency.com/danny-interview

2

LAND CLIENTS 2: BUILD AUTHORITY

Standing Out from Your Competitors
and Becoming the Obvious Choice
for your Ideal Clients

T he biggest thing that helped accelerate our agency from where
we were to multiple seven figures was a shift from just chasing
prospects to what we call, "inbound marketing."

When you shift from having to chase people to getting people to
come to you, everything changes.

*If you're going to get to the next level, you need to
have some inbound work in play.*

Clients come to you prepositioned to buy because they've been exposed to your expert status and they see you as an authority.

Because of this, your sales resistance drops.

As I made clear in the previous segment, there is a place for using cold outreach, especially in the early stages of your growth.

However, it makes a big difference if they've called you and said something like:

► "I've already seen what you did for these other plumbers. I want to hear what you could do for me"
► "I read your book"
► "I sat on that webinar, and you shared these five principles that really made sense to me"

When they come to you like this, you could expect more like a 30% to 50% close ratio compared to the 10% I suggested for cold outreach.

You will have plenty of appointments and you can get momentum and consistent growth.

This is critical. If you're going to get to the next level, you need to have some inbound work in play.

So, in my mind, to really get this working right, the objective is four to five new clients per month.

I think that's a sweet spot almost all of us should be able to hit.

I know a lot of guys doing a lot more than that, but at that level, you can get to seven figures or $83,000 per month.

To do that, you're probably going to need to book at least 15 to 20 strategy sessions per month.

Those are people who are scheduled for an appointment, and they are ready to go through your consultative sales process.

We'll talk more about the appointment process and how to handle those meetings in the next chapter.

If you can position yourself as the expert and flip the script from you chasing them to them chasing you, your business totally changes.

Your business really becomes a much easier and fun thing to do.

There are lots of ways to position yourself as the expert and I'm now going to share with you:

- ► 9 assets that can position you as the expert in any niche
- ► My favorite way to do that easily so that you can both nurture your existing database and make it keep growing

9 Positioning Assets

9 Positioning assets that can make you the EXPERT in any niche

- Keynote presentation
- Marketing Guide for that Niche
- Niche website with great content
- Case Study & Testimonial(s)
- Video based training / webinar
- The Book on Internet Marketing for that niche
- eMail Follow Up Sequences
- Podcast
- Print Newsletter

1. Keynote Presentation

The first thing is to develop a keynote presentation, which is just a thoughtful presentation on what somebody in that market should do to get better results online.

For example, if your target market is pest control, the keynote presentation can be: "9 things every pest control company should do to generate more leads online."

Do a presentation that hits those nine things – how they should have a great website, should get ranked, should optimize in a certain way, and so on.

When you develop that keynote presentation, you record and distribute it widely. You put it up on YouTube and you load it into some social profiles.

Then, you start to reach out to the associations, saying, "I've got this great keynote presentation on how to help your pest control guys generate better results online."

If you were to get in front of the National Association of your niche, you should be able to share your presentation and have the audience see that you understand their space.

This is a great foundational step. Everybody should have at least one core keynote presentation. Once you have that presentation made, it can be the baseline of all your positioning work.

2. Cheat Sheet / Marketing Guide for Your Niche

You could also make a cheat sheet or marketing guide, which is essentially the same thing as the presentation. "The 9 key steps for every pest control company to truly maximize their lead flow online."

If you're like me, I like to speak, I like to be on video. So, you can use your keynote presentation and record it to create your guide. Or if you prefer to create written content, then you can create a guide and then use that to make your keynote presentation.

3. Niche-specific Website

A niche-specific website is not, for example, "LocalAgency.com". That would be far too generic. However, "PestControlMarketing. com" would be a niche-specific website as it narrows in to a specific field of expertise. It's a website that is filled with all the content in it specifically built and written for that single niche. On my website, "PlumberSEO.net", the whole website is about how you generate better results as the owner of a plumbing or HVAC business online. I go into lots of great information on how to claim their directories and how to generate online reviews and lots of case studies.

Everybody should have at least one core keynote presentation

You want to have a website set up so that when people think, "I'm interested in you," and they go to look you up, they see that you've got a lot of detailed information out there that speaks directly to them, and they see you as the expert.

Ideally, you should have a niche-specific website for your company. However, you could also have it as a subsection on your site if you've already got a strong brand.

I'd say if you're coming from the ground up, set up a niche-focused website, i.e. PlumberSEO.net. Fill it with great content on how to get their website ranked, how to optimize for reviews, and how to leverage page search. Make it a hub of great information that brings people into your funnel and you'll have laid the groundwork for establishing yourself as the expert while attracting new clients at the same time.

4. Case Studies and Testimonials

Case studies and testimonials are probably the number one play you can use to build your authority.

Putting out good content makes you an expert in theory. However, when you can show results of actual people within your niche where you have gotten them tangible results—now that's the ultimate authority.

So, as you start to roll out case study content, your expert status grows exponentially.

5. Web-based Training and Webinars

Video-based training and webinars are just taking your keynote and recording it and inviting people to it on auto-play.

6. Book for Your Niche

In our niche, we've got our book, *How to Triple Your Sales by Getting Your Internet Marketing Right for Plumbing and HVAC Contractors.*

This is one of the most powerful positioning assets that we ever did. Why? Because ultimately, who's the expert? The expert is either the person at the front of the room or the author of the book.

If you can say you wrote the book on internet marketing for that niche, you're the expert. And you can own that expert status.

To me that's the ultimate status. You can use that book to get speaking opportunities.

7. Email Follow-up Sequences

With email sequences, you are making sure you're following up automatically when somebody registers.

8. Podcast

I'm a big fan of running podcasts. The easiest type of podcast is an expert interview. Everyone likes to hear about people like themselves.

So, if you're working with hotels, you could do a podcast where once a month you interview a successful hotel operator.

It's nothing to do with your service, it's just, "How did you grow your business? How do you generate your leads? How do you keep your hotels full?"

Ask them seven or eight questions that you ask everybody, and you'd be surprised how much that positions you as an expert. Even if the people you are interviewing are not clients.

I've got two podcasts. Firstly, there's my "Plumbing & HVAC Marketing Show," which is where I interview multi-million-dollar plumbing companies from across the country. That gives me great positioning.

Then I have my "Plumbing & HVAC Marketing Podcast", which is where I just share ideas and tips.

9. Print Newsletter

We send out a printed newsletter every month to the people in our space.

They get it in the mail. People don't get stuff in their mailbox anymore. So, when you send something in the mail and you show up consistently, it's a great way to position yourself as the expert.

These are all great strategies you can use to become seen as an expert.

There are lots of things you can do, but many of these would be over the top for anyone who is right out of the gate.

Now, think about this for a moment—what are just two or three of these expert positioning things that you don't already have in place, that you could do and can get done within the next week?

These are all positioning assets. However, I've got a great process that I'll share in a moment that you can tap into to make this surprisingly simple.

The Key to Building Relationships

Inbound marketing is not just about having content out there that positions you as the expert. It's also about having a database of prospects that know, like, and trust you.

A few years ago, I was at the GKIC Info-Summit where Frank Kern was speaking and one of the key things he said was:

"The money is not just in the list, it's in the relationship to the list"

So, it's not just about having a list of hundreds or thousands of people, it's about having a list of people that know, like, and trust you.

You've got to develop systems and processes to build those relationships over time. And, you must be producing good content consistently so that your stuff can be found in cyberspace and so that you can consistently nurture your list.

We've built our list using all these mechanisms that we talked about in the previous chapter. We've joined the association, we do

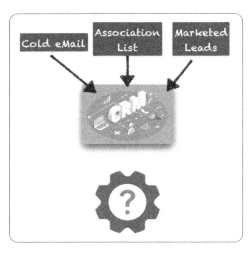

our outreach, and we cold email our prospects. Ideally, all of this ends up in a database like Infusionsoft or ActiveCampaign or Agile CRM.

However, here's where most agencies fail. They've got a database of people that they've reached a couple of times and now it's just sitting there stagnant.

Remember, the money isn't in the list, it's in the relationship to the list.

So how do you work those relationships? You've got to interact with these people at least two to three times per week.

The reality is, if you're emailing your database, let's say once a month, with deliverability the way that it is, and with attention the way that it is, only one-tenth of your database would ever see anything that you send. So, you must be reaching out to them on a consistent basis.

A gamechanger for me was Andrew Cass in one of our Mastermind sessions. He said, "So, you're selling to these plumbers, how often are you emailing them? How often are you reaching out?" And I was like, "I don't know. We do like one email a month."

He said, "No momentum is going to happen with one email a month. If these people are going to move from not knowing you to knowing you, liking you, trusting you, wanting to hire you, you've got to have more touches happening on a very consistent basis."

And they need to be value-added touches. You need to move away from the cold type, "I'm looking to work with one person in your area" or "Can you use two to three more a month?" to adding value.

You have to be giving them information that's of benefit, "Here's how to set up your plumbing website to get ranked on page one." or "Here are three strategies we found that work well to get 10X on your page search campaigns."

You must give them content they would want to consume and is actually good.

So, we've got to interact with them a couple of times a month. We've got to make sure that those are value-added touches, and then we've got to nurture that database and frequently offer help.

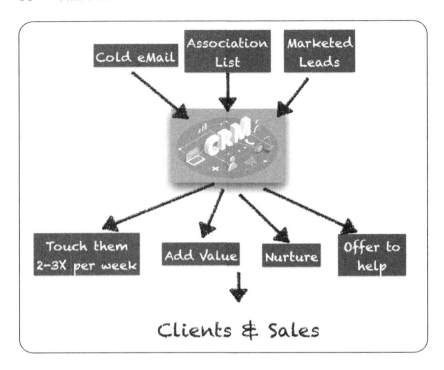

Nudging Them Forward

As you're giving this information and as you're positioning yourself as the expert, you need to tell them, "Look, if you need some help with this, if you want our team to implement these strategies for you, we'd love to jump on a one-on-one."

If all you do is put out value-added content and expect them to connect the dots, sometimes they will, but most of the time they won't.

You need to help them transition by going from "I gave you this great information" to "Now let's talk about how we can do it for you."

It's got to be a symbiotic relationship between adding value and asking for opportunities to do business.

When you do this consistently you will begin to see things start to come up.

However, doing it consistently is a challenge and that's why I want to share one of my favorite shortcut strategies with you.

The Shortcut to New Content Every Month

Here is my number one tactic to shortcut this entire process – monthly topical webinars.

SHORTCUT

MONTHLY TOPICAL WEBINARS ARE THE ULTIMATE CONTENT LEVER FOR AGENCY GROWTH

The fact is that using topical webinars on a monthly basis is the ultimate leverage for driving your entire content machine.

And by this, I don't mean one keynote presentation webinar. I mean, something new and topical on a monthly basis.

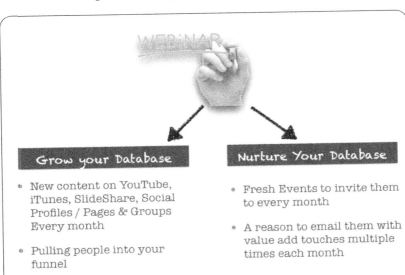

Grow your Database

* New content on YouTube, iTunes, SlideShare, Social Profiles / Pages & Groups Every month

* Pulling people into your funnel

Nurture Your Database

* Fresh Events to invite them to every month

* A reason to email them with value add touches multiple times each month

Webinars are a great way to shortcut this process because:

You can use webinars to grow your database from an inbound perspective.

You can use webinars to nurture your database and move people from "He cold emailed me" to "He added value to my world."

1. How Webinars Grow Your Database

Webinars help you grow your database, because when you create a webinar it can be syndicated in a lot of different ways.

Let's say you do a webinar about how to get ranked, and then you do a webinar about how to get reviews, and then you do a webinar about how to set up a website for a pest control company: you can take all that content and use it in a range of places, such as:

- ► Load it up on YouTube
- ► Put the slides on SlideShare
- ► Post the recordings on social media. Post not only on your personal page, but also on your business page, in groups that you control, and post to groups that you participate in that are relevant to your niche
- ► Post the recorded version of your webinar on your website as a blog post
- ► Take the audio from that as an MP3 file that is now a podcast episode that can sit on iTunes and other podcast sites
- ► Transcribe the audio through a service like Rev and post it as a blog post

By doing this, you can pull people into your funnel every single month.

They can see that new webinar that you did last month, find it useful, and then start to follow you, or they opt-in and they get into your database. You can then nurture the database by rolling out fresh content every single month.

In this way, one longer presentation becomes five or six pieces of content all pulling people into your funnel.

Let's say I do a webinar on the "5 Ways To Generate Better Results Online". That might be a 45-minute block of content. But there are bullets within that content.

▶ The first bullet might be, "Create A Website That's Built To Convert"

▶ The second bullet could be, "Optimize Your Website So It Ranks In The Search Engines"

▶ The third bullet could be, "Put A Strategy In Place To Get Online Reviews"

You might have two or three more bullets. Those little blocks of content might be five to seven minutes. You can cut each little piece of content after the fact and load that up as a separate video.

The whole webinar ends with, "If you've found value in that and you'd like more ideas and strategies, I've got this great checklist…," and you send them back to your website to download the checklist.

That worked well for me. Initially, I had one webinar. Sliced it up multiple times, and I just kind of saturated YouTube with all sorts of great content about how to market a plumbing company online, and it was all just split from a one-hour-long presentation.

You don't have to do all that manually. You can get a virtual assistant who knows the process and they can do it all for you.

2. How Webinars Nurture Your Existing Database

In terms of nurturing your existing database, running the webinars gives you reasons to contact them a few times a month.

What happens, in most cases, is you get this database and you rarely touch it. Once in a blue moon, you send an email out to them, and it's essentially a waste of time.

However, when you start running webinars and are sending them out consistently, it changes everything because now you are interacting with them a couple of times a week with value-added content.

You nurture them, you offer your services to them, and that's where you can start to get a steady flow of new clients coming in every month.

When you do a live webinar, you get their attention. You now have a reason to email them multiple times, and you have a reason for them to give you their undivided attention for even just a moment.

A live webinar is another reason to email them multiple times because nobody gets offended if they get two or three emails saying, "Hey, I've got an event coming up, I'm going to be talking about how to get your plumbing company ranked on page one." The following email strategy for notifying your database of your live webinar will give you 3 reasons to email them several times:

- ► The invite to the webinar
- ► The reminder right before
- ► The replay after the event, "In case you missed it…"

What I've found is, if you don't have a reason to email them, the database goes cold, but, if there's a value-added reason, you can be in their inbox frequently without annoying them.

By adding value on a consistent basis, you can drive multiple streams of new content.

The bottom line is, one webinar per month gives you a reason to interact with your database three times – that database that you need to nurture. And it gives you at least six pieces of content that you can roll out on a monthly basis.

You don't have to make this super complicated. You can simply take one webinar and that can really generate a lot of activity.

Webinar / Content Lever

- A **reason** to email your list with an offer...multiple times
    - Invite to the webinar
    - Reminder before the webinar starts
    - Replay after the webinar
- Drive's multiple sources of **NEW** content
    - Live Webinar
    - YouTube video with recording of webinar
        - BONUS - Sliced up elements of the webinar
    - Blog Post on your website with replay & transcription of the webinar
    - Audio from webinar for Podcast Episode
    - Slides from webinar in PDF on SlideShare
- Leverage Social Media to drive registration & replay consumption

Having only one webinar per month can drive your entire lead generation and content machine.

This is the main marketing activity I do every month. I commit to doing one webinar and decide on a specific topic.

I promote it, I show up, I do it, and then my team syndicates it.

So how do I come up with the content topics for my webinars? I'll discuss this next.

Choosing Webinar Topics

So, what should you do webinars about? Just do it on topics that are relevant to your prospect base.

Since you are reading this book, chances are that you're a student of the game. You sit on webinars; you're hearing from other experts. You probably go to conferences.

If you take that great information and you apply it to your niche, whatever that may be, you'll have the ability to really stand out. All you need to do is show up and provide great value.

Some of the topics that work well for us are:

- ► Annual plan
- ► SEO Formula
- ► Guide to Google Maps
- ► How to optimize for maximum conversion
- ► How to get ranked
- ► How to get online reviews
- ► How to tap into social media

The list goes on, and on, and on. There are all kinds of cool topics that you can do this on, and the more targeted to your niche, the better.

Updating Your Content

One cool hack on this is that once you've come up with an inventory of say 10 to 12 topics, you can recycle those just by putting a new year on the front of it.

People don't want to know about the general SEO Strategy. They want to know about this year's SEO strategy.

They don't want to know about how to generate pay-per-click results. They want to know what's working right now in pay-per-click results.

To update your webinars, you just need to make a few tweaks to your slides, and you call it the 2019 or 2020 version. You now become prolific.

It's not hard to come up with 12 webinars. That way, you can do a new webinar every single month that would be of interest and value.

For many of you, in doing just three or four webinars a year, you're going to position yourself as the expert. You're going to be the thought leader in that niche. Clients will come to you as the expert, followed by opportunities, such as to present at the front of the room in big conferences where your clients and prospects are aggregated.

Webinars are very powerful, however, many people don't do them because of several obstacles. Next, I'll discuss what many of these obstacles are and how you can overcome and avoid getting trapped by these pitfalls, yourself.

The Surprising Secret About Webinars

One thing I see that stops a lot of people doing webinars is they spend a lot of time vexing over the perfect webinar:

- ▶ "I would love to do webinars, but I don't like the way I look on camera"
- ▶ "I don't think I'm smart enough to say something intelligent"
- ▶ "I don't think my slides are going to look right"
- ▶ "I don't have the right set up or lighting"

So, they spend a ton of time trying to have the perfect webinar, that they don't ever do the webinar.

Here's the strange reality that should help people like that act.

The reality is, most people don't attend the webinar.

If you promote your webinar to 1,000 people and 60 people register, you're going to have about 10 people that show up. So, most of them won't even watch the webinar. And, even more important, your best prospect? The person you really want?

That seven figure business owner who will make this decision and jump onboard with you right away—will not attend your webinar.

They just don't have the time. They don't really care that much – but, they will register for the webinar.

Now this next part is the craziest insight. If you don't get anything else from reading this book, just remember this takeaway: It's not about the webinar. It's about the promotion of the webinar.

If you can send interesting emails that catch your prospects' interest enough to say, "Wow, I want to know about that topic," you can still create new appointments with highly qualified prospects on a monthly basis, even if they don't attend your webinar.

The seven figure business owner who will jump onboard with you right away—will not attend your webinar.

You can do this, provided you set up an appointment funnel system correctly, which I'll show you how to do next.

HACK - HOW TO GET GET QUALIFIED APPOINTMENTS EVEN IF THEY DON'T SIT ON YOUR WEBINAR

Creating an Appointment Funnel and a Shortcut

For years, I did webinars. I would promote the webinar and the "Thank You" page would just be, "Thanks for signing up. Please put the date on your calendar."

I'd then send a bunch of emails. I'd have some people show up, and I'd maybe wind up with one or two appointments.

And that was fine. I'd get a few appointments and a couple of them turned into sales.

But when I understood the reality that my ideal customers were signing up for the webinar because they were interested in the topic, but they didn't have time to attend, I changed my approach and my business was transformed.

One of the most important things I'm going to say on this topic of using webinars and positioning yourself as the expert is to make sure you offer a shortcut to an appointment.

This is the hack to get qualified appointments even if they don't show up for the webinar.

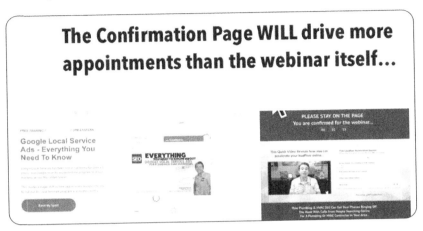

Here are the steps in the process:

1. Promote the webinar on whatever the topic is, e.g. "How to generate leads with local service ads"
2. Send them to a landing page to register
3. On the landing page, in addition to the confirmation of the registration, have a video saying:

   "Thanks for registering for the webinar, it's going to be awesome.

   If you're like most pest control companies, you like to understand how it works, but you really want somebody that knows what they're doing to do it for you.

   If that's you, I want to offer you the opportunity to schedule a time with me where I can talk about how we can execute this for you in your business."

4. In the confirmation email for people who sign up, mention, "You're confirmed but let's schedule an appointment."

You take them straight from registering for the webinar to scheduling an appointment.

When we started doing that, the number of sales we got from our webinars multiplied by 10.

Because the fact is, most people register for webinars but never sit in on the webinar. They want to watch the replay, but they rarely watch the replay.

However, you've got their undivided attention right when they express interest in attending and you can move them right then to an appointment. For us now, the number one strategy to generate sales and leads from a webinar isn't the live webinar. It's not even the recording of the webinar. It's the page that they get to right after they register for a webinar.

When we started doing that, the number of sales we got from our webinars multiplied by 10.

Just to illustrate this point, I did a webinar on local service ads a couple of months ago, and this is pretty typical for me now. 193 people registered, 58 people filled out my pre-assessment form, and 19 scheduled strategy sessions.

So, here's what's important:

► Don't overthink the webinar
► Don't overthink the presentation skills
► Promote the webinars
► Get the clients that are interested onto your calendar

That's a massive insight. Believe me this shortcut is a gamechanger.

This is a very cool hack to get people to schedule appointments right out of the gate.

In addition, if you've got capacity and you are doing cold outreach, there's no reason you can't call everybody that registered for the webinar. These are pretty warm people. They registered and showed interest, so get them on the phone and have a conversation.

Nevertheless, bear in mind, although 90% of them aren't going to even sit in on your webinar ever, it's still a good thing to show up and do your best. This is because some people will attend, and some people will eventually buy from it.

That also forces you to create good content that you can use in other ways.

Who Takes the Appointment?

Of course, once you've got the appointment, what happens in the one-on-one is very important. We'll talk specifically about that in the next chapter.

However, a question I'm often asked is, because I'm the face of the company, does everybody do business with me? Do I handle everything?

People do business with people they know, like and trust – and they want to deal with the expert. And a lot of times there's a personality tied to that.

So, if they're seeing me on the slides, they're seeing me on the website, they're thinking Josh Nelson is the number one guy in internet marketing.

You might be shocked to know that they come through that process to schedule a one-on-one call and that appointment is taken with my director of business development.

Then, once it's sold, it goes to an account manager who launches the relationship.

At one stage I thought, "I'm the one on the videos, I'm the one that's all over the place. They would only want to do business with me."

However, that is not necessarily the case. Our process has changed over time in this area, and has worked well for us at each stage:

► At first, it was me selling it and it was me launching it
► Then it was me selling it and somebody else launching it
► Then it was me promoting it, somebody else selling it and somebody else launching it

Obviously that process depends on you and the size of your business, but I'd say don't feel you have to do every stage in the process.

Promoting the Webinar

When it comes to promoting the webinar for maximum impact, again you want to do email but don't stop there.

If you have the opportunity to send social posts to invite people, that's great. If you can, run a promoted post, especially to people on your retargeted list so that they know about it. Doing this can create a sense of omnipresence in your prospect's world.

Don't forget, you've got this database of people that you're marketing to. There are several ways they can be hearing from you as you promote your webinar:

► You're in their inbox because you're emailing them about the webinar that's coming up and the replay
► They're seeing you because they like your page on social media
► They get a social message from you or a VA acting as you
► They're seeing your ad on Facebook about this webinar

Retargeting is a cheap way to remain top of mind with your prospects and get nearly omnipresence, where they feel like you're everywhere.

However, the reality is that you appear to be everywhere simply because they were on your list or because they were on your website. Retargeting strategically positions you and your promoted webinar with top of mind awareness to your database.

Rinse and Repeat

Once you have a few webinars created plus a process to consistently create them and a strategic way to send them out to your database, then you just rinse and repeat with these 3 steps:

- ► Roll out new webinars on a consistent basis
- ► Promote them to your database
- ► Syndicate them online and via social media

This is the best shortcut to nurture your database, position yourself as the expert, and put out new content on a consistent basis that makes you prolific in pretty much any niche.

Two Types of Learning

Here's something that's important as you work through this book and for any type of learning. There are two types of learning:

- ► "Just-in-case" learning
- ► "Just-in-time" learning

Just-in-case learning is the worst thing that you can do. That's like, "Okay, Josh taught me about webinars. So, I'm going to learn how to run a webinar and how to promote a webinar, and I'm going to learn about it just in case someday in the future I do a webinar."

Let's face it, we've all done just-in-case learning with the best intentions and have never done anything with it. You should move everything you do to just-in-time learning.

Just-in-time learning is, "I've got a webinar scheduled for February 17th. It's in my calendar. I've blocked it. Now I need to make sure I get some emails out and I've got the webinar coming up, so I'd better set up my slides. I've got people registered for this webinar, so I'd better get myself ready to do a webinar."

Then you hustle and just-in-time – as in, just before the webinar— you know what you're doing and you pull it off.

If you can get yourself into just-in-time learning, you'll move everything in your business faster.

Now that you have a steady stream of clients you are going to attract, the next element we'll look at is mastering the sales process you should follow to close the prospects that are going through your funnel.

 SEVEN FIGURE ACTION

Complete the following steps:

▶ Commit to monthly webinars.

▶ Map out your next three months' worth of webinars. Over the next three months, what are three webinars that you will conduct?

▶ Block a date in your schedule.

Case Study: Leveraging Webinars to get clients coming to you

A great example of implementing these strategies to land clients is Jeff Fisher from Local Childcare Services. When he joined our program, he was a generalist agency. He was kind of stagnating. He was struggling to land clients consistently.

He jumped in, he bought into the concept of choosing a niche and decided to focus on local childcare facilities. He also committed to selling recurring, monthly services. He had previously been selling $175-a-month services, and he upped it to $1,000 per month.

Cold outreach was one thing that Jeff just didn't excel at—he's an amazing entrepreneur, team leader & excels at operations. He's not the kind of guy that's going to bang on the phones.

The key thing that moved him forward was starting to do webinars, and he started doing webinars every single month.

So, he latched onto this whole idea, "If I can do one webinar, I can get it split up. I can do it on a consistent basis. I get some raised hands; we can start to land some clients."

He started doing it, and what happened was, he was promoting the webinars and people weren't showing up.

I think Jeff would tell you, he doesn't have a lot of presentation confidence, it's not his favorite thing to get in front of people and present. But he committed to it, and he did it.

People weren't showing up for his live webinar, but it forced him to create the content, record it and syndicate it.

It was the follow up after the webinar and the content that got added to cyberspace, that started to generate a consistent lead flow of clients.

He only gained one new client immediately. Every other one came somewhere in the next 30 to 45 days.

That became his little rule, every webinar counts for 30 days of generating new leads.

He started landing, on average, two to three new clients every single month from the webinar strategy.

That's what moved him forward to over 100 clients and to the point where he was able to sell his agency for a great profit last year.

He's now one of our Seven Figure Agency success coaches who helps me train other agencies on how to implement these strategies and how to move their businesses forward.

**You can listen to a full interview with Jeff Fisher on
how he built, grew & sold his agency by going to**

https://www.sevenfigureagency.com/jeff-interview

3

LAND CLIENTS 3: SALES MASTERY

Making Sure As Many Ideal Prospects As Possible Say Yes to Your Offer at the Right Price

Once a prospect has expressed interest in your services, you need to take them through a specific process to help them decide to sign up with you.

I'm going to share with you here what I feel is the ideal sales process for selling local internet marketing services.

I've learned that most people, when they have a prospect interested, simply rush in with a "canned presentation" and just tell them all the cool things they're going to do.

What I have always found much more effective is what I call "consultative sales," where you first take time to find out about their problems and then show how you can help them solve these specific problems.

When you get those calls and when you get those opportunities, what I'm going to suggest is that you don't dive right into, "Here's what we do and here's how we do it and here's how much it costs."

Instead, we want to follow a four-step process, as follows:

1. **Initial Call:** A brief conversation to set up a further meeting
2. **Pre-meeting Research:** Preparation you do to allow you to present specific ideas at the second meeting
3. **Review Meeting:** A longer meeting where you demonstrate that you understand their needs and show them how you can help
4. **Close / Follow Up:** You ask for the business, either at that meeting or in a series of follow-up contacts

Let's look at each of those steps in more detail.

Step 1: Initial Call

In that first call, when they have contacted you, you want to ask a couple of questions about their business and what they're trying to do.

Then you schedule a follow up meeting.

The way I frame it is by saying, "Thanks so much for your call. I appreciate the opportunity. Let me get some information about you and your company."

What you've done in that environment is you've moved from being a salesperson to being a consultant.

Then I say, "Rather than me just telling you exactly what we're going to do for you, I'd like to do some due diligence on my end. I'd like to review your website and review some of your online marketing strategies.

Then, when we talk again, either a little bit later today or a little bit later this week, I can show you where I think you're doing well, and where I think there's room for improvement.

We can then identify what we can do together based on where you're at today and where you're trying to go. Does that make sense?"

It's highly likely they'll say, "Yes, that makes a lot of sense."

What you've done in that environment is you've moved from being a salesperson to being a consultant.

You are offering to add value and show them how you can help.

So, I always suggest that the first call, be only an initial call where you gather information and then state, "Let's schedule a time now, where I can demonstrate my findings to you." This allows you to be prepared for the next call so you can tailor your conversation specifically to them and show them how they b will specifically benefit from your services based on your research.

Step 2: Pre-meeting Research

As I stated earlier, when you get to the Review meeting, you want to be able to show them that you know something about their company. You want to be able to show them where they have issues or problems.

Remember, in the absence of a problem, it's very hard to get somebody to buy anything.

So if you can show them, "Here's where the problems are and here's what will happen in your business once you solve these (for example, you will see more traffic, more calls, more leads, more profitability), you can get them excited and prompt them to start doing business with you.

However, before you can do that, you need to do some research. That requires a bit of work on your part but, with the right tools, it does not need to be difficult task.

There are four main areas you need to look at:

► Website basics
► Keyword research
► Current ranking
► Local issues

To be able to show them the issues with their current online marketing strategy, you need to use some tools. I've recommended some here. I'm not saying these are the only tools, but these are the tools that we've used and they're pretty effective for us.

Website Basics

You're going to want to start the meeting by doing a review of their current website, so you just need to take a look at their site and look out for basic issues such as:

► Is the phone number in the top right-hand corner?
► Do they have a clear call to action? (For example, "call us now at this number" or "click here to schedule an assessment")
► Are they leveraging personality? (For example, do they have authentic pictures of the staff and the owners and the office or are they using generic stock photography?) Of course, it's my opinion that authentic imagery is going to work and convert better than stock photography
► Do they have good content for each of their different services?

Make a note of the major things you will talk to them about.

Keyword Research

To do the keyword research, I'm going to suggest that you start with your imagination.

Regardless of whether you're dealing with a dentist, a roofer, a chiropractor or any other local company, you can use your imagination to say, "What would I type in if I needed a dentist?" So, it might be something like dentist, dental services, tooth pain, etc.

Then you'll be able to take that small list and plug it into the Google Search Tool.

To use the Google Search Tool, simply type in your keywords and submit. Google looks against the AdWords data and will come up with a list of the most commonly searched keywords along those lines and put it into a list for you.

You can then whittle that down and come up with your own short list of the "money" words or the most searched words.

If you're selling local internet marketing services, the foundation of that is knowing both:

► What people are typing into Google, Yahoo and Bing when they need your type of services
► What needs to be done to make sure that you're showing up in the search engines for those searched keywords that are going to drive traffic

So, it's incredibly important that you spend the time needed to figure out what those most commonly searched keywords are.

From there, you can use a tool like Merge Words, which then gives you the ability to take those 10, 15, 20, 30 keywords and combine them easily with the cities that the prospect operates in.

It is just a keyword combiner where you can:

► Put in column 1 all the different core words that you've found
► Put in column 2 all the cities that your prospect serves

You end up with a list of, "their city + this," "their city + that," "their city + this" and you'll have a nice list of keywords geo-modified for their area.

So, you'll have your most commonly searched keywords combined with those cities, and you'll have a compiled list of locally concentrated keywords.

You then take that list and put it back into the Google Search Tool, to figure out which of those geo-modified keywords has the most search.

Current Ranking

The next step is you're going to want to assess their current rankings for those keywords. To do that, you can put them into a ranking tool like BrightLocal, which is great for local businesses.

RECOMMENDED PRE-MEETING RESEARCH TOOLS

▶ **Google Keyword Research Tool:** Helps you figure out the most commonly searched keywords for your particular prospect.

▶ **Merge Words:** Lets you combine those keywords with the cities that the prospect operates in.

▶ **Bright Local:** Shows you exactly where they rank on search engines for all of those different keywords.

▶ **Local Site Submit:** Shows the issues with their current marketing efforts.

First, you set up the company with their website address and their phone number and all of their information. Then you just plug those keywords into the report.

What will happen is it will search Google, Yahoo and Bing and give you a corresponding number between 1 and 50. Number 1 is page one, spot one. 50, being wherever it is further down the list for each of those keywords that you came up with for the client.

Depending upon what program you're on, it will hit Google Local, Yahoo Local, and Bing Local and pull ranking reports and say exactly where they rank on those search engines for all of those different keywords.

This is a great way to paint the picture, "Would you agree these are the most important keywords?" "Yes".

You simply follow up with, "Well, based on my research, and my due diligence, your company's not ranking on page one. That means there are people looking every single day for these services and you're not showing up. That, I think you would agree, is a pretty big problem. Because there's prospects in your market, in your space, looking for what you do and they're not finding you."

Local Issues

From there, you're going to want to be able to say, "Here are the reasons your website's not showing up in the search engines."

That's where you're going to set up a search report on Local Site Submit.

Again, other tools do this. However, I've found Local Site Submit to be a very nice tool that presents a great report that will say, "Here are the most important online directories. Are you in them or not? Here's how you're referenced across the web."

What Local Site Submit does is it will look at all of the citation sources for the client. It will look at their online reputation and it will give you a nice customized report to say, "This is why your website's not ranking."

Of course, as you do that, it becomes very easy to roll into: "Here's what we can bring to the table through our services; here's how we'll bridge this gap."

We know that the key to getting ranked in the Google Map listings, especially is:

► Lots of citations

► Consistency of the name, address, and phone number

► Number of online reviews that the company has

The Local Site Submit tool generates a report to show where there are deficiencies along those lines.

And of course, you'll run that report and it will give you that data and give you a percentage of visibility score.

It will say how optimized their Google listing is, as well as their Yahoo listing, and their Bing listing.

Ready for the Meeting

This gives you a great arsenal of tools so that when you go into that meeting with the client, you won't just be talking at random.

You'll be speaking specifically about the due diligence you did.

► You researched the keywords

► You figured out what the most important keywords are

► You ran a report to figure out where they rank in the search engines for those various keywords: Some of it's good, some of it's bad, and you can show them why

► You ran another report that shows how they're being seen by Google across the web: which shows what the specific issues are with how they're being perceived, and why they're not ranking well in the map listings

Now that you've done your due diligence, you're ready to go into that second follow up call with a lot of confidence and be able to say exactly what you can do, in more detail.

Next, I'll discuss how that second live meeting should go.

Step 3: Review Meeting

This meeting could be on a phone call or in person at their office or yours, but for time efficiency, we usually suggest doing them on a web-based meeting.

We want to drive this with a three-part process:

Build Rapport: Spend some time getting to know the person by asking some questions to understand what their goals are. Again, you're being consultative and you're building a little bit of rapport along the way.

Review of Findings on their Current Approach: Show them the problems with their current strategy so that you can show them exactly what you can bring to the table.

Present Your Solution: You need to demonstrate your ability to solve their problems. You should be able to say, "You're here, this is where you want to go. This is why you're not there. And here's what we're going to do in order to bridge that gap."

Build Rapport

The first thing to do is to build rapport and ask questions. You don't want to dive right into your assessment findings and say, "Here's what we're going to do and here's why it's great."

You still have to spend the time and ask questions and get to know the customer and get to know what their goals are.

You start just talking with a little bit of natural conversation, "Hey, you have a beautiful office from the photos", etc. Find something that is natural for you to start a conversation.

Then ask something a little broader, "Tell me a little bit about your background in the business." Let them start to talk about who they are, what their company's all about, how long they've been in business, whatever information they want to share.

Don't make this beginning part feel like an interrogation. It needs to be natural, needs to be a business conversation.

For that reason, I don't want to give you a list of 10 questions. But you do need to spend some time getting to know them and asking some questions.

Ask them about how they are currently marketing their company. If you're going into the right prospect, either via live meeting or in person, you're going to be dealing with a company that is well established.

You don't want to be dealing with the folks that have no interest in investing in marketing.

In my mind, that's one that does at least $1 million per year in revenue. And it does marketing and they believe in marketing already. You don't want to be dealing with the folks that have built their business just on word of mouth and have no interest in investing in marketing and marketing strategies.

This question really will, therefore, help you determine if there's a good fit. Ideally, you would do this over the phone in advance. "Tell me a little bit about how you're marketing the company today?"

If they're saying things like, "Oh, we're in the Yellow Pages. We do a lot of pay-per-click advertising, we've got billboard ads and we run radio ads," those are indications that that company invests money in advertising and probably is a great fit.

If they're saying things like, "We're just word of mouth," you might jump straight to the chase on this and say, "Hey, our programs range between $1,500 and $2,000 per month. Is that going to work for you? Do you think that's something you would consider if the value's there?"

That's just to save yourself the time and energy.

Again, you can ask questions like, "Tell me about how you're marketing your company today? How many technicians? How many employees? How many dentists?"

Ask about whatever makes sense, just to get a sense of the scope and the size of their operation.

Then you can ask, "Where are you guys at currently, in terms of revenue?" The reason you're asking this, is so that you can find out where they're at today and then you can ask the follow-up question, "What's your goal in the next 12 months?"

Another way to phrase this question is, "If we could teleport into the future, and everything went according to plan, where would you like to see yourself in the next 12 months?"

Look for an answer in terms of customers, in terms of revenues, in terms of whatever metric is important to them.

Asking these question gives you the ability to build a little bit of a relationship with the customer, where they start to feel like you care about them and you're asking questions and you're trying to learn about them, as opposed to just sell your wares.

This is a quote that I've always found to be powerful:

"They don't care how much you know until they know how much you care."

And asking these questions gives them that sense that you care. You can then shift into reviewing your findings.

Review of Findings on Current Approach

From there, you're going to review your findings with them. "Here's what we found as we reviewed your website. Here's where the issues are."

The presentation of your findings is fun because so many people go to their office or talk to them on the phone and just launch straight into a sales presentation without doing any due diligence.

They haven't done any research, and they don't have anything of value to bring to the table. On the other hand, you've done your due diligence.

And now that you've done the research, what I recommend, as you start to review your findings with your prospect, is to walk them through their website.

So, say, "Mr. Jones. Do you mind if we get in front of a computer? I've looked at your website, I've looked at your online marketing strategy, and I'd love to share what I've found and where I think there might be room for improvement. Is that okay?"

Which, of course, it is okay.

If you're doing this on a phone call, you'll say, "Hey, Mr. Jones, can we do a shared screen session where you can get online and see my screen? That way, we can be looking at the same thing together." If you're in their office, you'd say, "Hey, let's jump on a computer."

So, what you do first is you pull up their website, walk them through it, and point out any issues that you might see, as we discussed earlier.

This is just allowing you to talk about their website. It's showing them that you reviewed it. Then point out some of the good and some of the bad about their site.

Now, you don't want to say, "Hey, this is the worst website I've ever seen." So, always try and point out something good. "Hey, you know what? It looks like you guys spent a lot of time thinking through this content. There's a lot of good stuff here, but I think there's a lot of room for improvement, as well. Here are some of the things that I've found that I think could be better."

From there, you're going to want to walk them through the keywords that you developed and where they're ranking for those keywords.

You can say, "We did the due diligence. We spent some time researching what the most commonly searched keywords are in your area for the services that you provide, and this is the list that we came up with. Would you agree that this looks like a pretty strong list? I've also got the search volumes associated with this and found the keywords that are going to be most important. Then, we plugged that information into a tool that helps us isolate where you're ranking on Google, Yahoo and Bing – where almost everybody goes when they're looking for these types of services. This report shows you're showing up for some of them, but for some of the most important ones, you have no ranking at all."

When you show them this, they will most likely say, "Wow. There are keywords here that people are typing in that I'm missing out on."

From there, you walk them through the local search findings report.

You'll need to tell them what this means, "Here's why you're not ranking for these keywords. You don't have enough citations. There are inconsistencies between your name, address, and phone numbers. You don't have enough online reviews," whatever the case may be.

You have the opportunity to show them what needs to be fixed with their online marketing strategy.

Now, you know they want to get more business and grow their revenues and they've already expressed their goals to you.

Then you've, in turn, showed them how they're not maximizing on potential opportunities in terms of rankings, leads, and calls which translates to less money for their business than they can be making.

From there, they're readily open and eager to hear the solution.

Present Your Solution

This is where you get to present your solution. Not on the initial call, but on the second call, after you have researched and presented your observations, instead of just diving straight into the solution on the first call. If you skip step one (the first call) and step two (the research) and just dive straight into your solution, it's probably going to fall flat.

However, if you spend the time in the front end to show them what they are missing as far as opportunities, then you explain, "Here's what we're going to do…we're going to get into your website and we're going to create these pages, and we're going to make sure it's optimized correctly. Then, we're going to get in and we're going to make sure your name, address, and phone number are consistent. As well as, make sure that you're in all the online directories across the web. We're also going to put a strategy in place to help you get more online reviews from your real customers, so that every customer gets an email after service and they can quickly write a review of your services. Then we're going to take over your blog and we're going to start updating the blog for you on a weekly basis, so that you have consistently, fresh and relevant content. Then we're going to do strategic link building to build inbound links back to your website, which all of this helps to make your website more authoritative so that it can rank better in the search engines. As we start to rank better for those keywords, all those words I showed you that you're not ranking for on this report are going to begin to move up in the search results. You're also going to get more visitors to the site, and you will start to get more calls and leads. As a direct result, you're going to see more revenue and more profitability in your business."

Then, you talk about whatever different packages you offer that fit their solution.

When you present it this way, you can expect a lot of interest from the prospect.

Step 4: Close / Follow Up

The final step would be to follow-up and close. You want to try and ask for their business while you're on the assessment call.

If you go through all of that and you say, "Well, I hope this was interesting. Do you want me to send you a proposal and we can talk again later?" you're not going to close a very high percentage. So, you must make sure to ask for their business at this point.

If you're doing it live and in person, you're going to close a relatively large percentage. If you're doing web-based calls and web-based meetings, the close-ratio will probably be a little bit lower.

In that case, you want to make sure you've got a process where you're following through and you're closing those deals over a one to two-week period, after the initial presentation.

At the time of the meeting, here are a couple of pre-closes you can use.

First, you can ask, "So, how does this sound in comparison to what you had in mind? Can you see how once we get your website content listings and reputation factors right, you're going to get more calls, leads, and business?" And they will ideally respond, "Yeah, absolutely. This is great. This is better than what I expected."

Or you could ask, "If you had to rate your interest in moving forward on this between a scale of one to 10, with one being not interested at all and 10 is you would like to get started right away, how would you rate it?"

This is a great question because if they give you like a seven or an eight, then you know that some things need to be addressed. "Thank you, Mr. Jones, for that feedback. So, you're at a seven, what would you need from me, to move you from a seven to a 10?"

At that moment, they might say, "I think I would just need to see a couple of your client success stories" or, "I'd like to talk to one or two of your clients" or, "I need to make sure that those keywords are right."

They're going to let their objections bubble to the top and then you can address those head-on and ask for their business.

Another option is to say, "Well, this sounds great. Let's get started. Would you prefer to use a credit card or a debit card?"

Now that your prospect is interested in getting started with you and your program, let's discuss the follow up sequences that will get you higher conversion rates.

Hot Lead Sequence

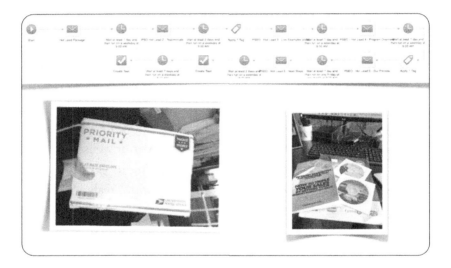

So, we have what's called a hot lead follow-up sequence after that presentation on a two-week timescale where they get:

- ► An email with a complete overview of the program
- ► A video of me, the owner of the company, explaining what our program is and what's included
- ► Two or three emails with video testimonials of customers saying that they've used us and had a great experience
- ► A "Here's what you can expect in the next 90 days, as we work together" email

If they didn't buy right on that second call, we say, "Well listen, we only work with one of your type of business in any city. And right now, we're proactively marketing to the other companies like yours in this market. It's going to be on a first-come, first-served basis. I'm not trying to create false scarcity. But the fact is, we feel like it's a conflict of interest to work with two or three or four companies in this market. We feel like we'd be competing against ourselves, and we don't feel like that's in the best interest of our clients. So, we only work with one. And of course, we are the experts in this space. So, there's a lot of interest in what we do. We are marketing to the other guys in your area. Can we agree, one way or the other, to decide on this by the end of next week?"

They'll probably say, "Yes." If they say, "No," then they literally have no interest and you can close that opportunity and just move on.

But they'll likely say, "Yes" and you then say, "Okay, great. Well, here's what I'm going to do. I'm going to send you a proposal. I'm going to get you testimonials and additional case studies. Let's put on the calendar to decide one way or the other by Friday of next week. Fair enough? Great."

By creating an end cap to your opportunities, you'll know what you've got something in the pipeline that's legitimate versus you just chasing your tail.

Your close ratio on these folks will be much higher because you've created scarcity and you've created a deadline where they must decide.

If you've created enough value and you've shown them where the issues are and how to solve them, then you'll find that you get a pretty high close ratio.

So, that's the consultative sales process. It's not super complicated. Remember:

► On your initial call, you want to schedule an assessment
► On the assessment call, you want to show them the pain and give them the solution
► Then you want to make sure you're following up and that you're closing those opportunities into new business

In the next segment we'll look at how you can deliver service that makes clients want to stay with you.

 SEVEN FIGURE ACTION

Based on what you have learned in this chapter:

► Design and script the initial call

► Identify the process and resources required to conduct the pre-meeting research

► Create a structure for the review meeting

► Script and outline your close / follow up

Case Study: Landing clients with sales process mastery

Matt Coffy runs a digital marketing agency based in New Jersey. He's been in the agency game since the early 2000s and tried just about everything in the book to build a successful business. He started doing direct-to-business work (local business & everything in-between) and grew to about $70K in monthly revenue. It was great, but it was not consistent. He'd get a big project that helped him to pay some bills, but it was not recurring, so the money was gone almost as quickly as it came in. He'd done a lot of work to position his company, Coffy Marketing, as the go-to agency in New Jersey. He even got the website ranked on page one for a lot of competitive keywords like, "New Jersey Digital Marketing", "New Jersey SEO", etc., which helped generate leads & sales. However, they were all over the board: from doctors to auto shops, and eCommerce to med spas, so his team was constantly needing to reinvent the wheel.

With that being the case, he had to do most of the thinking and strategy work himself and was getting burned out. He could not continue to sell new clients & maintain the client base, so of course, his revenue fluctuated wildly from $30K one month to $70K the next month. Without any consistency of cash flow or the ability to systematize his business due to the variation in the types of clients he worked with, he knew something needed to change.

His next approach was to start a white label agency providing internet marketing services to other agencies that did not want to do it themselves. This bumped his revenue, but only further exasperated his operational issues.

He was working 60+ hours per week, Monday through Sunday. He also had a big offshore team with very low profit, and a general feeling like he was just stuck. Finally, he went back to the drawing board. He decided that he would focus on a vertical that had worked well for him over the years—med spas. He set up a new division called "Practice Bloom" and focused all his attention and effort on that. With one vertical & a systematized service offering, he was now able to grow his revenue, build his team & systems, and ultimately get to over $110K in monthly recurring revenue (and growing). Matt stuck with it and now runs a seven figure digital marketing agency.

You can listen to a full interview with Matt Coffy on how he built and grew his agency by going to

https://www.sevenfigureagency.com/matt-interview

PART TWO

DELIVER RESULTS

4

DELIVER RESULTS 1: CHOOSE MODEL

Design Your Business for Speedy Growth and Maximum Profit

One of the most important foundations of your seven figure agency is choosing the right business model.

There are several elements to this, which will determine how quickly and comfortably you can reach seven-figure status.

I've experimented with different approaches and made a few mistakes along the way, so I want to share with you some principles that will help you avoid the waste of time and money that can delay your success.

I believe the lessons fall into three key areas:

1. **Follow the Rule of Five Ones**
2. **Use the Recurring Revenue Model**
3. **Choose the Right Niche**

Let's look at each individually:

1. The Rule of Five Ones

In the Business Fundamentals section at the start of this book, I talked about something that I had found useful in building my seven figure agency—and that was the Rule of Five Ones.

As I mentioned, I got this from Taki Moore, of Million Dollar Coach (I'm a big fan of his), who got this from Clay Collins, who set up LeadPages and who has now built multiple seven-figure agencies in very rapid sequence.

Taki asked him, "What is the key to your success and how were you able to grow so quick?" Clay's answer was, "The Rule of Five Ones."

From my experience, I believe it's important to understand the Rule of Five Ones if you want to know the fastest way to grow your digital marketing agency.

1 Target Market / Niche

1 Lead Generation Strategy

1 Conversion Mechanism

1 Program

1 Year

Here's a quick reminder of how they apply to a marketing agency, though the concept is the same for just about any business.

- ▶ One target market
- ▶ One lead generation strategy
- ▶ One conversion mechanism
- ▶ One program
- ▶ One year

Let's look at each a little more closely.

One Target Market

When you run a digital marketing agency, anyone who runs a business could be your prospect. It could be the roofer, the AC contractor, the dentist, etc. It could be anybody.

What often happens is that you look at your local market and you serve whoever you can get.

So, you're jumping from one client to the next, one type of opportunity to the next, and one prospect to the next. That was my experience at ReachLocal and it was hard work.

My agency now serves plumbing and HVAC contractors. That's our one target market.

When you choose that approach, it means you will probably have to work outside your immediate geographic area, but there are advantages to that.

When I moved from being a generalist to being a specialist in one particular market, everything accelerated.

I was able to put together marketing that made me magnetically attractive to that group.

I was able to put together systems and processes to serve that type of business and get it done well and knock it out of the park for them.

Once we got the ball rolling in the plumbing and HVAC market, anytime I got somebody outside of that niche, it put the brakes on the whole operation. It really slowed things down.

To whatever extent that you're in multiple markets, you're slowing down your ability to really accelerate your agency growth.

The fact is, everybody I've worked with that's had real success and growth is in one niche. And they focus hard on that.

For example:

▶ Allan Hillsburg was a generalist and decided to focus on funeral homes and went to seven figures

▶ Brian Stearman started focusing on lawn care maintenance companies and built a seven figure agency in about 12 months

I can tell you example after example, but, for every one of those success stories, there are a dozen other companies who decided they could be more profitable by focusing on a geographic area familiar to them as opposed to choosing a niche.

These people never get past $250,000 per year.

In my experience, whatever markets you serve, I can tell you that having one specific target market will make your life exponentially easier, and your marketing exponentially better.

One Lead Generation Strategy

There are many ways we can generate new prospects, such as:

▶ Cold email
▶ Cold calling
▶ Networking
▶ BNI meetings
▶ Facebook advertising
▶ Pay-per-click advertising

However, the fastest way to get results is to have one great lead generation strategy dialed in that you can do consistently.

You don't want to be running 20 different things that are below average or average. It's much better to have one that's fleshed out and consistently generates leads for you. Doing it this way allows you to focus on getting it nearly perfect.

Make sure to choose one that you can scale. For example, relying on a specific networking event may provide great results when you are small, but you'll eventually run out of people to talk to.

Being focused on a specific niche also makes it easy to identify which lead generation method works best to reach them. For example, what delivers results with dentists may not be best for carpet cleaners.

One Conversion Mechanism
The conversion mechanism is how you sell the client and once again there are lots of options, for example:

► Webinars
► Live events
► One-to-one selling
► Strategy sessions

Again, you want to become great at one of them and focus on that.

In our business, it's usually one-on-one selling. What tends to work best is getting people on the phone or in a Zoom meeting and taking them through a consultative sales process.

You want to become great at taking somebody from interested, to doing monthly recurring business with you.

One Program
To make growth fast and easy, you should offer one core program to your clients that can deliver the results they are looking for.

As I stated earlier, it should not be a la carte, for example: a website here, web hosting there, and a custom application over there. You can have some variations of the program for specific circumstances, but you should not be custom building everything you get.

You want to have one clear picture in your mind of what you want to offer a client and exactly how you are going to get them what they need.

You want to be able to speak to the prospect and say, "This program will give you the results you are looking for."

Then you sell that, with potentially one or two variations.

A lot of people get stuck with trying to sell something initially that's less expensive and then try to upsell into a higher ticket offer. In theory, that makes a ton of sense. That's just not the way we did it. I've seen a lot of people get stuck where they're selling a lot of the low-ticket stuff and not managing to upsell.

Having just one program is a big challenge for a lot of agency owners because they want to sell ad hoc, or they want to sell customized work.

The truth is if you're going to scale to seven figures quickly, you need to have one clear idea of what you sell and how much it costs. Then stick to that for a year.

One Year

The key for each of these elements is to focus on them for one year. You need to allow enough time in each element to become great at it before you consider adding anything else.

Some people say, "No problem. I can focus on a niche. Yeah, I can focus on lead generation strategy. Sure, I can sell via the phone or via Zoom meetings. I'll even stick to one program."

But when I say it's got to be for a year, people begin to have doubts and say, "Wait, I thought that was for a few weeks or a quarter."

We all have shiny objects syndrome and it makes it difficult to stick to things when we don't see instant results. It is common to want to switch between niches often to find one that "works", but the key is consistency.

You need to allow enough time in each element to become great at it before you consider adding anything else.

The big problem is that a lot of people decide on a niche or a service to provide and then two or three months in, they feel like they need to change things up again and they decide to go down a different path.

Clay Collins said, "To the extent that you add another number to any of these, like if you try and do two niches, or you're trying to sell two programs or five programs, you multiply the complexity, which makes it that much longer before you can truly get your business to the next level."

Yes, over time, you may want to experiment with a second method of lead generation, for example. However, wait until you've become great at one before you try another.

My Experience

People ask if I used this model to get to seven figures.

The truth is, I did. I just didn't realize it at the time. It wasn't like I discovered the Rule of Five Ones and decided to follow it.

When I worked at ReachLocal, I was selling anybody I could get. However, I realized that when I met with a dentist, for example, and I'd taken him through a consultative sales process, they'd say, "What other dentists have you worked with? Can you show me some examples?"

So, I was like, "Man, how much easier would it be if I only went after dentists?"

This prompted me to decide to focus on one niche once I had a couple of clients from that niche.

We started off with a couple of niches, such as dentistry, roofing, and AC contractors, and then we landed on plumbing. Once we had a couple of clients, we started to become great at getting inbound leads.

We also became great at having one product, which was the equivalent of a $2,500 a month internet marketing service, though it was a lot less at the time.

That was the mechanism that accelerated our growth and I am confident the same approach will work for you.

2. Use the Recurring Revenue Model

The next fundamental element of the Seven Figure Agency Model is getting the finances right.

There are two keys to this:

- ► It should be recurring income only
- ► You must charge high enough fees

Recurring Revenue Only

In my initial business, which I talked about earlier, I would sell a website and I'd get 50 percent upfront: $500 today, then $500 once the website was done. There was also a fee of $50 a month, but it never really amounted to much.

Even if I sold seven clients one month, the next month I'd have to go out and sell seven brand new clients just to be at the same level.

On the other hand...

If you're selling monthly recurring fees, and the number's large enough, that's where you get some significant momentum.

There are various ways to reach $1 million in annual revenue, including:

- ► One client that pays you $83,000 per month
- ► Eight or nine clients that pay you $10,000 a month
- ► 41 clients at $2,000 per month
- ► 83 clients at $1,000 per month
- ► 166 clients at $500 per month
- ► 830 clients at $100 per month

Now the reality is that there are not many businesses out there paying $83,000 a month unless you're selling to very large companies. The $10,000 a month level is not entirely crazy, but you may not be able to build your business on them alone.

While the top one is hard, I would say the bottom is the hardest.

If you think you're going to convince 830 people to pay you $100 per month then you're going to be on that wagon for a long, long time.

1 Client	$83K per month
8-9 Clients	$10K per month
41 Clients	$2K per month
83 Clients	$1K per month
166	$500 per month
830	$100 per month

That's a mistake I see a lot of people make. They think that they will be able to build more if they have a lower monthly payment.

And that was the mistake I made at my agency. I thought, "Well, I'll just sell to a bunch of people and I'll get them at $50 a month in residuals on hosting. Eventually, I'll have this big monthly recurring income."

It never happened, and it won't happen anytime soon. I've had a lot of people come to our program and say, "I'm going to sell something for $500 a month" or "I'm going to sell something for $299 a month" and they think like this because they believe they will eventually have enough clients that the number will be significant.

What I've found is that it takes almost as much energy to sell somebody a $2,000-a-month program as it does to sell them a $200 program.

You'd be much better served to land fewer clients at a higher dollar amount, to really expedite the growth of your agency.

The sweet spot is between $1,000 and $2,000 per month.

If you can charge more, great. I'll explain in a moment how we charge a higher fee than that, but it may not be the easiest place to get started.

If you can land three to five clients per month at $1,000 to $2,000 per month, you can get to seven figures in 12 to 24 months.

Mathematically, five new clients per month, paying you $1,350 per month, gets you to seven figures in just 12 months.

My point here is that, if you charge enough in monthly recurring, it can be significant enough to help you grow quickly.

No Projects

In my opinion, recurring revenue is the only way to go. If you do some project work, even if it is big project work, you take one step forward and one step back.

You restart every single month. "I got this big $50,000 project. It was great." Yes, it was $50,000, but that $50,000 is deposited and it goes away relatively quickly.

If you have a mix of project work and recurring work, the project work capitalizes on your time. You get sucked into the project and you struggle with focusing on building the recurring revenue.

If you focus instead on just the work that generates a recurring monthly fee, that number grows, and it will continue to snowball every month.

This will help you get to the place mentally where you're envisioning your business by focusing on the monthly recurring revenue, so don't waste your time on project work.

Also my advice to you is, don't accept check payments. Personally, I don't accept check payments. If you have to go to their office and say, "Hey, write me a check for the $2,500 fee," my experience is you may get the check the first time and the second time, but the third time they will probably have excuses, "Oh yeah, I'm out right now. Come by tomorrow" or "I'll mail the check out to you."

The consistency of your revenue is never there, and believe me, it will drive you nuts. We got to the point after our second year that our business model didn't allow for check payment. If you want to pay by check, we'd rather not have you as a client.

Charging Enough

So, I think your monthly fee needs to be at least $1,000. I'll tip my hat to Lyn Askin on this for saying…

If you're not getting $1,000 per month, you're probably not solving a big enough problem.

You either aren't great at getting your clients results, or you just don't have confidence in what you're doing.

I can promise you; $1,000-plus is going to get you there a lot faster than $1,000-minus.

A great example of this is John Tate. His company is Agency Marketing Machine, and he focuses on insurance agencies.

I spent years in a mastermind with John. He was a generalist agency. He was selling project work and some recurring client work. He was in fashion, e-commerce and basically all over the place.

Month after month, we'd get together and while my business was taking off, his business was just kind of stagnating.

He was always reinventing the wheel and he was always wondering why he didn't make any money.

We finally convinced him to focus on a niche, and he decided on the insurance agency niche.

Then he built a recurring revenue model and he focused on selling one core program.

The right business model really makes all the difference in the world between struggle and rapid success.

Over the past three years, I've seen his business just blossom from complete struggle to right now doing about $1.5 million this year.

His agency is consistently doing over $130,000 per month in recurring revenue.

Deciding on a niche was just a massive gamechanger for him, and that's what I want for you. I want you to get the right business model, because it really makes all the difference in the world between struggle and rapid success.

Some keys to making that happen are:

►   Believing in yourself
►   Finding the right prospects
►   Being able to prove the value

Believing in Yourself

A lot of agency owners don't believe that businesses will pay them $1,000 or more a month. That was me when I started. However, when I started working at ReachLocal, the minimum cost was at $1,000 a month. We simply were not allowed to sell to anybody for less than $1,000 per month.

That was a massive mind shift for me. I was like, "What do you mean? There's no auto repair shop down the street that's going to pay me $1,000 a month."

I had to come to grips with the fact that, yes, they will.

As I went through the training processes, I took note of the other sales reps – and ReachLocal had about 3,000 sales reps across the country. They had to sell five clients every single month, and if they didn't hit that target, they were out of a job.

There were a lot of people selling those types of clients, month in and month out at $1,000 or more per month.

I can tell you that you have a much better chance of getting 83 clients to pay you $1,000 a month than getting 166 clients to pay you $500 a month.

The biggest difference here is the amount of effort it takes. You must sell double the number of clients to make the same amount of money.

It takes as much energy to sell someone on paying $100 a month as it does to sell them on paying $1,000 a month.

Some would say it takes more energy for the lower level guys, because once you get them, they're needy and they'll drive you nuts.

Finding the Right Prospects

An important predictor of success is finding prospects who are within your realm of reasonability. Make no mistake, they're out there. You've just got to make sure you're getting to the right types of prospects.

Getting started can be a major challenge. However, as you grow, and scale, and start to dial in your ideal client, it's not that big of a stretch.

If you're dealing with companies doing $750,000 to $5 million per year in revenue, and they're already spending money in other various advertising mechanisms, they're used to spending.

They've got a $10,000 or $20,000 a month budget. You're not going to get all of that, but you can get a share of it if you can show them intelligently, "I'm going to take $2,500 of that and I'm going to invest it in this, this and this and here is the expected return on investment."

There are certain things you need to look for to make sure a prospective client is big enough. It depends on your market, but it may be something like how many trucks they have or whether they have a full-time receptionist.

Of course, it's partly a personal confidence thing. When I started out on my own, despite what I'd learned at ReachLocal, even $1,000 at that time felt like a big number for them to pay me to manage their stuff.

So, that's where I started. As we got clients and got them results, my confidence level built, and little by little, we increased our business.

Proving the Value

One of the things to bear in mind is that you have to become good at actually generating the results. You have to become good at being able to show them that while they may be paying $5,000, they are going to get tangible things in return. You should have a means of showing them exactly what you have done for them. This is very feasible for you, and very palatable for them.

So, the sweet spot is at least $1,000 to $2,000 per month.

If you could get people in that range, there are tons of prospects willing to pay that.

You can generate a great measurable return on investment if you know what you're doing and you get your service offering dialed in right.

Another thing regarding pricing and value is to work backward a little bit because there is a certain cost to fulfill.

If you're positioning yourself as an authority in the niche and as an expert in digital marketing, you are going to want to hit it out of the park for them. You need to be charging enough to deliver on that.

You need to become confident with what you're bringing to the table and how much revenue you're going to bring for your clients.

You'll feel more confident knowing that you're going to bring them another $10,000 or $20,000 a month in revenue at a decent profit margin of 30% or 40%, depending upon your niche.

Knowing this should help it feel like no problem to ask for $2,000 or $3,000 a month.

How We Justify $2,500 a Month

Our minimum fee is currently $2,500 a month. At that amount, we are dealing with larger clients who are already spending at a certain level and they're able to see all the social proof of the great results we've gotten for our other clients. They get it.

For $2,500 a month, we offer a pretty comprehensive service. This is what's included:

- ► We launch a new website for them
- ► We create pages for all their services and all their cities
- ► We optimize it for the most important plumbing & HVAC related keywords
- ► We do local SEO, claim their online directories, and log in for them on a consistent basis
- ► We run their paid search, pay-per-click advertising campaign (The spend is on top of that)
- ► We set up a YouTube channel

▶ We also give them a reputation management tool to help them get reviews on a consistent basis

That's our core program at $2,500 a month and we've got an ultimate program where we also do re-targeting and social media posting, etc., as additions.

Delivering Value Fast

One of the things we changed in the last three years is that we were essentially an SEO company.

So, we would build a website, optimize it, do the links, do the citations, and put in the review system. It would take us about two months to get the website launched and the ball rolling.

Then, SEO, being what it is, would take three to six months before the website starts to rank for their key terms and they start to get an increase in calls.

As a result, there were struggles of our clients asking questions like, "When am I going to get my ROI? When is the phone going to start to ring?"

Upon recognizing that, we morphed to a package that was SEO and PPC, over the last couple of years.

As a result, within the first two weeks, we could get landing pages and a pay-per-click campaign running so that phone calls would start coming in for our clients right away during the early months.

That way, they would at least break even in the first two months or so.

And then the tail, that is the SEO portion, starts to pick up soon after and we're getting a great return on investment over the lifetime of the relationship.

Seven Figure Bottom Line

The bottom line is this—if you can land five clients per month paying you $1,350 a month or more, you can have a seven figure agency in just 12 months.

If you're a little bit slower than that, you can get there within 24 months. That's not that many clients.

If you're charging $2,500 a month, that might only be three clients a month.

So, you can see how this is feasible. It's feasible if you put in the work and select the right niche.

3. Choose the Right Niche

Now, I want to unpack why to choose a niche, how it's going to make your life easier, and outline some of the key things you want to look at when choosing a niche.

Why Choose a Niche?

One of the key reasons to choose a niche is the simple fact that everyone wants to work with an expert in their type of business.

Whether you're dealing with the roofer, the dentist or the chiropractor, when they're trying to choose the person that's going to help them with their website, their SEO, their social media or their lead generation, they want somebody who's the expert in their specific field of expertise.

They want to work with someone who has experience in their niche: someone who has built websites like that before and someone who has actually gotten results for similar businesses.

When you become good at your particular niche, it's going to make your life easier to land clients.

It's going to be easier to sell. It's going to be easier to close business. It's also going to be easier to fulfill and systematize your process.

What we experienced in the past was that, when you jump around, it's more difficult to build your business.

Our business today is built to serve plumbing and HVAC companies and that has many advantages:

► We know what the keywords are

► We know the pages we want to have on the site

► We know the wording we want to use on the content to make sure it converts well

► We know the directories that our clients should be in to get the best results

► Our project management system is loaded up to follow the exact steps needed

That's why we're able to handle more clients and scale our operation.

That is the strongest case for being in a specific niche. It's easier to attract clients and it's easier to close those clients once they come to you. It also aids the scalability of your business, because you systematize your processes.

You can become the best at generating results within your industry because you start to work with several companies in the same type of industry.

When you know the industry and you're testing to figure out what works and what doesn't, you can confidently say, "If you give me $1,000 per month, I'm going to get you a great return on investment."

I can say that with a high degree of confidence in my market because I've done it so many times, I've tested so many different things, and my team is just that great at it.

These are the reasons you want to be in a niche. I've found it to be the fastest and easiest way to accelerate the growth of your agency.

I could share example after example of agencies that were struggling and trying to find their footing. Agencies that were jumping from one industry to the next.

Then, after finally choosing and committing to a single niche, they had accelerated growth within their agency. That's what I want for you.

Now that we have discussed how important it is to have a niche for your business, let's focus now on how you can choose the right niche for you.

Keys to Choosing Your Niche

As you choose your niche, I want to draw your attention to the things you should be looking for in your selected niche.

This can apply at different stages of your development:

- ► Maybe you're in the early part of the process and you haven't picked a niche yet
- ► Maybe you've picked a niche already, but you're just not sure if it's the right one
- ► Maybe the one you started with wasn't the one you wanted

Whatever your situation, there are a few questions you need to consider about your niche to determine your chances of success.

Do they clump together or self-identify?

What I mean by self-identify is, can you create a website, a lead magnet, or a video where you name that group and they would say, "That's for me. This guy is talking to me specifically."?

For example, if you were to say that you create websites for roofing companies, then any roofing company would be able to self-identify with your company because you are speaking directly to them.

However, if you were to say that you create websites for contractors, then that description, though it sounds more specific than just any business, still falls under the category of generic. This is because contractors could be referring to roof builders, air conditioning contractors, general contractors, electricians, and the list goes on and on.

In our case, we serve plumbers and we can say that we have the complete guide to internet marketing for plumbers, and they recognize that it's for them.

However, that wasn't always the case. At one point, sometime at the beginning of our business, we decided we were going to not just be the plumber SEO specialist, we were going to be the contractor SEO specialist.

The idea was that the market for all home service-based companies would just open up and we'd have a very large group to pursue. We could then get plumbers, carpet cleaners, roof builders, so on and so forth.

We could get so many companies under this contractor SEO brand.

We wrote a book, The Complete Guide to Internet Marketing for Contractors. We had a podcast. We had a great website, all kinds of content. This was just going to attract the landscapers, the lawn care maintenance companies, and everybody else under the contractor umbrella. We could just expand from there.

What we found, however, was that contractor label didn't resonate with anybody. It was just off track.

Plus, we'd get occasional leads from here and there and occasional clients from different fields, etc. Nothing like what we get with our Plumber SEO content, because Plumber SEO speaks to one specific audience.

So, make sure that you're not going too broad and that you have a single, specific niche. A niche that, when you create your content and put your whole process in place, is going to resonate with your content and be able to self-identify with it.

Do they have a propensity to invest in marketing?

There are some niches who do not have the propensity to invest in marketing. Niches who never really had to spend money to generate customers.

An example of this in my mind, and I could be wrong because I've never tested it, are Certified Public Accountants, (CPAs).

There's lots of CPAs. Many of them are doing over $1 million per year in revenue. It seems like that would be a great niche.

However, the doubt I have with a niche like CPAs is that they don't have a propensity to invest in marketing.

Most CPAs are word-of-mouth centric. They get a client, and then that client refers them to somebody else. In most cases, they don't advertise in the Yellow Pages or in direct mail in order to generate new clients.

On the other hand, locksmiths, for instance, used to have huge ads in the Yellow Pages.

They all know the only way they get locksmith leads is by showing up when somebody is looking for them.

They're used to spending $1,000, $2,000, $5,000 per month in order to generate leads and generate calls.

So, make sure whatever niche you're focused on is the kind of niche that will spend money and is used to spending money.

What you want to avoid is having to convince people that there's a lot of people looking for their service online if they have never spent money to generate leads.

It's a much easier battle to say, "Hey, you're already spending $5,000 a month. Let me take $1,000 of that and show you how to generate leads via the internet."

That's better than trying to convince them that they should be spending money in that way.

I would also add to that, when you're choosing a niche, I find that business-to-consumer is an easier avenue because consumers tend to search on Google, whereas the CPA is business-to-business.

I'm not saying there's no one searching for it, but most people don't go on Google to look for a CPA. Most people tend to rely on word-of-mouth, such as by talking to their financial guy or friends, etc.

To re-iterate, there's probably not a lot of volume in many business-to-business searches.

With fewer people now using Yellow Pages in many markets, when you want to assess a niche and their propensity to spend money on advertising, tools like SEMRush are useful.

You can plug into different types of niches and see how much paid competition there is, what the average cost-per-click for their keywords are, and if there's a lot of competitors.

If there's a lot of people bidding on the keywords, there's a good chance that they have a propensity to advertise.

If there's a high cost-per-click, there could be a lot of potential there. Plus, if there's a lot of companies bidding on those keywords, that suggests they're used to spending money to generate leads via search and even via offline channels.

Essentially, you just want to make sure that they're spending money to generate customers and not just living off word-of-mouth or some other advertising channel that isn't online.

Are there enough of them?

The other thing you want to do is double-check to make sure there's enough business that exist in your niche. Don't waste time going after a market if there's only a couple of thousands of businesses that exist for a niche.

In general, you want to substantiate that there's at least 10,000 companies in the niche that you can go after.

An easy tool to use to determine how many companies are in a specific niche is InfoUSA. For example, if you are thinking that bankruptcy attorneys might be a good niche, go into InfoUSA, and either find the "CID code" or just enter, "bankruptcy attorneys" in the search field. It will list how many of them there are and how many of them are doing over $1 million per year in revenue.

This will help you gauge whether there are enough of these companies so that if you did become the dominant player, you could achieve your sales and revenue goals and have a sustainable business.

Is there an industry association attached to the niche?

This is probably one of my favorites and one of the most important factors in choosing a niche.

In almost every vertical that you can imagine, there are association groups. For us, it's the PHCC (Plumbing-Heating-Cooling Contractors) Association, which is national.

Then, there's one at each state level and there's one at just about every local level, as well. If you go to Florida, California, Utah, there's a PHCC. Then, in Florida, there's a Miami PHCC and a West Palm Beach PHCC. It's a very aggregated group of people.

You want to double-check in your niche whether there is an association that you could join.

I strongly encourage you to join an association in your niche. Then, leverage the fact that you're a member by requesting access to their member database. From there, you can market to this list of members for your direct mail campaigns, email campaigns, and webinars. It makes your life so much easier.

You can buy lists from a lot of different places, but the list you get straight from the association is the cleanest list you're going to get.

This is because the people on the list you get from the association have paid for membership and they're contact information has been verified. You can also get a full mailing address in most cases.

Next thing you want to consider is whether you can get involved in the association and if they have periodic events where they are coming together.

If they're meeting, there's an opportunity for you to get in front of them.

If they are meeting and you attend, there's an opportunity for you to get in front of them and then follow up with them after the meetings, so you will want to check to see if that's an option.

You must market hard in these things. You must prep yourself before you go to the ev ent, letting everybody know you're going to be there, putting out information. When you're at the event, you must interact with the people there. Then, afterwards, you must continue to market to them. Things aren't going to fall into place right away. There's a very good chance that the first event you go to, you're going to walk away with talking to very few people and make no sales.

Then, I think what happens often is a lot of people feel like trade shows don't work because they leave without closing any deals their first time.

Don't ever expect to go to your first event and come home with anything. It's about building trust over time.

I've seen a lot of companies like ours at these events. They come to one event and don't get anything, and then they never come back.

That is great for us because it's less competition, but if you don't continue to go to the events and market to them, you just ensure you never get anything out of them.

Another important thing to understand is that many of the people going to these events are specifically looking for help because they know this is a place of trust.

You are a member of this association, so they're coming, and they feel like there's a level of trust there. It's not just some guy who cold-called them offline and they don't know who they are.

A lot of times we go to these events and people come up to us and say, "I came just looking for an internet marketing company." These occasions are priceless, and these opportunities are completely missed if you do not continue to attend the events on a regular basis.

When we started going after the plumbing niche, I found the Miami Plumbing Association. It wasn't the case where I joined the association and then magically got a windfall of clients. It took invested time of planting seeds, and then one client turned into a lot of different clients in this space.

So, make sure that there's an association in the niche. It doesn't have to necessarily start at the national level. In our case, it started at just the micro-local level and grew from there.

Some Solid Niches

Just to get your creative juices flowing, I'm going to share some of the niches we've found to be very solid. These each have enough people in them, and they have the propensity to advertise.

I've found laying out a list helps somebody say, "Maybe I should try that niche." However, don't feel like this is the end-all be-all of lists. Definitely use this as a starting point to get the creative juices flowing.

I really feel like the right niche should almost select you based on your experience, your background and your communication style.

There's going to be certain vertical markets or niches that are just going to be a better fit for you than others.

However, these are some of the ones that I find to be good.

Legal

I like legal. They have the propensity to advertise and market in most cases. They're advertising on radio. They're advertising on TV. They've got billboard ads. They've got big ads in the Yellow Pages.

If you do the PPC search, you'll see on SEMRush there's a ton of people in legal competing for the top terms.

In the legal space, I think the following fields of expertise are great niches: bankruptcy attorneys, personal injury attorneys, divorce attorneys, criminal law attorneys, and traffic attorneys. These are all good because the transaction value is quite high.

If somebody needs these types of attorneys, usually they're looking online at some level. So, using SEO, pay-per-click, and social media advertising is very valuable.

Almost everything in your bag of digital marketing tricks plays well in the legal space. Again, the transaction value makes it work well, as well.

Home Service

Home service niches are tremendous. It's probably one of the best verticals because it's usually driven by somebody looking online and the transaction values are usually pretty good.

Going back to my days at ReachLocal, a $250 million per year digital marketing agency, ReachLocal had a lot of business in home services.

Some of my favorite niches in home services are:

- ► Kitchen remodeling
- ► AC repair
- ► Plumbing
- ► Landscaping
- ► Roofing
- ► Electricians

- ▶ Pest control
- ▶ Locksmiths
- ▶ House painters
- ▶ Commercial painters
- ▶ Floor installation
- ▶ Damage restoration
- ▶ Garage door installation and repair

That's just to name a few and they are not ranked in any order. They are just niches that I've seen where I know there's a lot of people and I know they have a propensity to spend.

I've seen other successful agencies targeting these niches and I know that there's a market to be tapped into. So, one of these might be the right niche for you.

In the home services area, every neighborhood in America gets a magazine or a couple of magazines to their house each month. It's called the Home Services Magazine. It's like 30 pages of all different home service companies. I browse through it every month.

You just look through there and see who's advertising in the full pages. Those guys are spending money. Those guys are spending upwards of $1,000 and $2,000 a month. Those would be great people to transition over to the internet.

Healthcare

There are lots of opportunities in healthcare, but I would urge you not to go too broad. Again, picking a specific niche is key. You might be tempted to just say, "I could do healthcare, and then I could call it Healthcare Digital Pros, or something like that." However, if you run a digital agency called, Healthcare Digital Pros, for example, that targets the entire healthcare space, you are going to wind up in the same place we wound up with when we tried to target the entire contractor space. The same also goes for the legal space.

You want to have a specialty within the specialty that's going to be your target. Within healthcare, it could be dentists. However, I will caution that I've had a bunch of people hop onto the dentist bandwagon in the past and found it to be extremely competitive.

There are lots of dentists, they have the propensity to invest and the customers do find them via search as well as insurance. However, there are a lot of companies going after the dental space. Everybody and their mother's calling the dentist.

I like dental. If you're smart and aggressive, it can work. I've personally sold a lot of dentists when I was at ReachLocal, so I know it can be done. However, it is also competitive and will be more of a challenge. Of course, within dentists, there are niches like orthodontic, dental implants, and cosmetic dentistry, as well.

Also, within healthcare, you have chiropractic, cosmetic surgery, weight loss centers, eye doctors, day spas, veterinarians, etc. The list goes on. They are mostly high transaction value. Even fitness centers, personal trainers, and gyms can be good niches.

Again, I feel like you want to choose something that's going to fit with you, your background, and your experience.

If you happen to have worked in one of these types of businesses, or you have a family member in one of these types of business, or you have experience dealing with companies that run these types of businesses, it can make your life a lot easier as you gravitate towards a niche.

If you're choosing something in the medical space, I would avoid going after any medical niche that is 100% insurance dependent. Such is the case for primary physicians, for example. They don't get a lot of searches as people would have to go off their insurance to do so in most cases.

On the other hand, people do search online for dentists and chiropractors so those two, and other niches like them, are good avenues. Just try to veer away from any insurance-dependent healthcare niches.

Automotive

The automotive space is another good option. This includes auto repair shops, auto body shops, auto dealers, etc. Bill Enross, who's a member of our program, has built a great business just serving auto body shops. This is a great niche. However, auto body and auto repair can be clumped together. I wouldn't necessarily think you need to just work with auto repair shops or just work with auto body shops.

Auto dealers, though, would be something separate. If you've got a background working with auto dealers, it could be a hugely lucrative opportunity, but it's going to be competitive.

Now, remember, this isn't intended to be a comprehensive list of niches out there. This is just the tip of the iceberg. Again, it's just to get your creative juices flowing and give you some good opportunities to explore.

We've had agencies come through our program that have selected a niche completely off this list and they have done fantastically.

Don't feel like just because I didn't list a niche that you're considering that I don't think it's a good idea. These are just some of the more obvious, low-hanging fruit opportunities.

What I want you to do is make sure that you select your niche and then 100 percent commit to it. Everything we do moving forward is built around the understanding that it all centers around that niche. You are now targeting this audience. You are going to structure everything around them. You should know what services you are going to provide, and your proposal is going to be written specifically with them in mind, as well.

This way, you can attract the right clients, close the business, fulfill their needs and then scale your service offering.

Moving Beyond Local

When you focus on a specific niche, you won't be able to rely on working just in your local market.

If you want to build a seven figure agency, there will be a limited number of companies in your area. This is especially true if you offer exclusivity, such as promising only to work with one client in that market in any area.

Part of our model is about offering exclusivity to our clients in specific markets. We now have one client in each major market across the United States.

A downside to this is that you lose the opportunity to have face-to-face meetings. The advantage, though, is that you can be a lot more time-efficient.

This is because local clients can suck you dry. If you've got to drive to their office, meet with them in person, and go through the monthly reports with them, you can't scale that model.

Even when we get a prospect in Miami, we don't meet them in person. I'm not going to drive all over town. They're going to expect me to come and pick up a check instead of giving me a credit card.

We prefer to conduct our business through Zoom meetings.

Zoom meetings help because people want to do business with people they know, like and trust. So, if you're on Zoom, you've got your camera up, they've got their camera up, and they feel like they get to know you a little bit and you can share your screen.

So, if you're going beyond your local area, is it better to go after a specific state, a specific region, or the country as a whole?

I believe it's better to serve the entire country or even go international.

Our first handful of clients were local, but now more than 90% of our clients are outside of South Florida.

However, one thing I will say is you might want to own your backyard before you try and go completely national.

When we started, we had a client in Fort Lauderdale, one in Miami, and one in West Palm Beach. They were all local, we could meet with them face to face.

You might find it's hard to get somebody outside your state as your first client.

However, once you have your first local clients, then people outside your area can see what you've done for your local clients. They can see that you got them ranking and that you got them more calls. Now you're an expert and you warrant the trust of that cross-state barrier.

So, you may want to stay local for the first couple of clients so you can build those relationships and develop your arsenal of experience and case studies.

That means, initially, you should use every strategy you can get. Sit in a BNI meeting. Go to a Chamber of Commerce. Find the people within your niche that you want to target.

Meet with them in person, get them to know, like and trust you. Have them become an advocate, but then continue to reach out and try and get clients outside the area.

When you go outside your area, a question that comes up is whether it's harder to get results for clients in some areas than in others.

For example, to rank somebody in Miami may be a lot harder than to rank somebody in Tupelo.

You have a choice between targeting highly populated areas like New York City, LA, and Chicago with millions of people, or targeting smaller areas like, Boca Raton and Doral with 100,000 or so people.

The competition that ranks someone for SEO in New York City may be harder than somewhere like Boca Raton or Doral or Melbourne or West Palm Beach, etc.

So, the question is whether it's better to go after the big city or a smaller area to get better results.

Initially, our thought was to go after the big metropolitan markets, such as Miami, Los Angeles, etc. The more people, the more opportunities, right? Though we were able to get some clients in those areas and still serve a lot of them, they are a lot harder to get results for.

> *What we found is our big opportunities, our big wins,*
> *came in populations of less than 200,000 people.*

You might think there are only 50 major markets in the United States, but there are literally 390 markets of less than 100,000 people.

That means there's enough companies out there for you to really run a good business. You can get them to rank well, dominate paid search, and you can win a very high percentage with a lot more opportunity than you realized.

Now that we've covered what type of clients to target and where to target them, let's look next at how to present the services you offer in the best way possible.

 SEVEN FIGURE ACTION

Spend a couple of minutes right now on identifying what you need to commit to change within your business model. In the chart below, there are two columns.

► The left column is your current situation.

How many niches? How many different programs? What's your monthly fee? How much project versus recurring work are you doing?

► The right column is your ideal situation.

What should your business model look like if you really want to accelerate and commit to seven figures? What do you need to change based on what we've just discussed that can make an impact for you?

BUSINESS MODEL	
Current Situation	**Ideal Situation**
► Niche	► Niche
► Program(s)	► Program(s)
► Monthly Fee	► Monthly Fee
► Recurring vs Project	► Recurring vs Project

Case Study: Getting The Right Model

Ray Malaski runs a digital marketing Agency called, "Web Launch Local". He is a serial entrepreneur that built and sold a Maid Service in the Michigan market. In the process, he learned a ton about Internet Marketing (SEO, PPC, Facebook Ads, and Web Development), so he decided to start an agency. Rather than going niche-specific, his initial plan was to cast a wide net and work with anyone who was interested in generating better results online. While he had landed some clients right away, it was a struggle to keep up with the work, because he was in so many different types of businesses.

Then, he joined the seven figure agency coaching program and got introduced to the concept of being "niche-focused". That would help him not only get more clients but make his business more scalable.

So, he took what he knew from his Cleaning Business, that he had built and sold, and started a new division called "Cleaning Clicks" and things took off from there. He went from only doing about $10K per month to $50K+ and growing with about 5-7 new clients per month. Ray is well on his way to building a solid seven figure agency.

You can listen to a full interview with Ray Malaski on how he built and grew his agency by going to

https://www.sevenfigureagency.com/ray-interview

5

DELIVER RESULTS 2: PACKAGE AND SYSTEMATIZE

Design Your Offer In a Way that Makes It Easy to Deliver and Sell

The core of your business is the service you deliver and the revenue it generates for you.

The way in which you deliver that service is crucial for your ability to attract clients, get them great results, and grow profitably.

So, in this chapter, we're going to look at putting together your service offering and getting clear on what you're going to be selling to your clients, how you're going to get the work done, what you're going to charge, and how you are going to profit from it.

It's important to map these elements out in advance because it's one thing to say you're going to go out and land clients in your niche, and then another to go out and actually start talking to prospects.

If you don't know what you're going to sell, how much you're going to charge, or how you're going to collect payments, then you're probably not going to have the confidence to have those conversations in the first place.

As we go over these key elements, I'm going to unpack exactly what we sell our clients, what the deliverables are, how much we charge, and how we present the services.

I'm going to give you that information with the thought that you can go ahead and tweak that and modify it for your specific niche and for your specific needs.

Of course, I am aware that not everybody wants to do SEO, pay-per-click, and web development exactly the way we do, and I also realize that there are certain niches where other services make more sense, such as Facebook advertising or funnel development.

So, while I know a lot of people want a proven model that they can follow, don't feel like you have to do it exactly the way we do it.

We are going to cover our process in the following steps:

1. **Developing a service that your ideal clients want and that delivers results**
2. **Delivering it efficiently so that they are satisfied, and you make a profit**
3. **Pricing it so that your clients buy, and you can meet your financial objectives**
4. **Presenting it in a way that makes it easy for people to sign up**

Developing the Service

When it comes to developing your service offering, I like to make sure that you're thinking along the lines of selling a complete solution as opposed to piecemeal work.

The illustration I like to use is selling the holes, not the drill. People don't go to The Home Depot and look for the best drill that has 10,000 RPMs per minute and has all these cool specifications.

They just need a hole to be drilled into their wall. They could care less about how it gets done.

So, that's what I'm talking about with you. As you go to position these services in the marketplace, just remember that we do have lots of tools in our tool belt, such as:

► SEO
► Pay-per-Click advertising
► Mobile websites
► Social media
► Retargeting

However, all the client really wants is more calls and more leads on a consistent basis.

As we've discussed already, I've always advocated for getting a monthly recurring fee that's large enough to encompass the complete solution that they really need to help them get more leads, more calls, and more customers.

As we've already mentioned, it's a good idea to keep in mind the Rule of Five Ones and keep your product offer very simple.

So, let's drill down on the service offering.

As I mentioned, I'm going to paint the picture of what we sell to our clients now and what the key elements are.

You can choose to take all of it and run with it. You can choose to decide to do some elements and not others. Remember, this is simply to help you customize your service offering.

The core elements in our package are:

- Website with content, proper optimization, conversion elements, and lead capture form
- Onsite Search Engine Optimization (Title Tags, H1 Tags, and good content)
- Authority Development via:
  - o Citation development (online directory listings)
  - o Content development (blog updates)
  - o Link building
- Reputation management (help them get more online reviews, showcase their online reviews, and deal with negative reviews)
- Pay-per-Click management to generate leads out of the gate and control lead flow
- Tracking and measurement
- Social media marketing (more expensive option)

Let's look at each of these elements in more detail.

Website Creation

For us, the offer really starts with rolling out an updated version of the website for them.

In most cases, especially for our ideal client, it's likely they've got a website, but it's probably not very good.

- It's not optimized
- It's not user-friendly
- It's not conversion-focused

We, therefore, lead with, "We're going to roll out a new version of your website that's built to convert and that's properly optimized. It's going to work great on mobile phones, and it's going to be the hub where all of the leads and customers that come to your organization are going to land."

This must be good, and so that's really where we start.

Onsite SEO

From there, we conduct onsite search engine optimization, such as updating title tags, H1 tags, meta descriptions, etc. – all the basic SEO stuff.

As it relates to the service offering, what we always tell our clients is that we want a good website that's going to convert, but that's also going to rank well in the search engines.

For home service businesses like ours, what we find is that having pages for their services gives them a competitive advantage from an SEO perspective. So, think about the typical website's pages configuration – Home, About Us, Our Services, Coupons, and Contact Us.

Where we go deeper is within the Our Services pages. So, as you think about your niche, think about the different services that your client performs.

For example, for a dental office within the dental niche, they've got dental cleanings, teeth whitening, Invisalign, braces, etc. If those are the services this particular dental office offers, we tell them we're going to optimize it for all the different keywords and we're going to create pages for each of those different services.

Then the place we also go deeper is in geographic service areas. We find most of our clients serve between a 30 and 45-mile radius, and so they have a main city, like Miami, and our main website is anchored around the main city, such as, Miami plumber, Miami plumbing services, etc. That's the Home page and that's the Service pages.

However, in that 35-mile radius, there are lots of little cities and sub-towns, so Kendall, Hialeah, Palmetto Bay, Pinecrest, Miami Beach, etc. There's usually 20-plus.

We try to focus on the top 10 cities in their service area, and we create pages for each one of those with unique content.

So ultimately, we want pages on their site for each of their services and each of the sub-cities that they operate in, especially if it's a service-based business.

That might not apply quite as well for a retail company like a chiropractor or a dentist. You might have to come up with a different mechanism for those niches.

Authority Development

Now we've got to get this website so that it has enough links and it has enough authority to rank well in Google and Yahoo! and Bing.

The tendency is to over-complicate this and think you've got to do a million-and-one things such as build a ton of links.

I'm going to share with you what we do in order to optimize our clients' sites, and it's probably a lot more simplified than you might expect.

▶ **Citation Development** is adding them to Google, Yelp, Angie's List, and Citysearch, all of the major online directories.

We use Yext for this, as well as BrightLocal. We like Yext because it has the API of the most important online directories and the speed at which we create it or update it to the time it actually goes live is extremely quick.

When we were doing it manually, it would take much more time. Even if we logged in and claimed a specific listing or modified it, there was often an approval process or some type of timeframe to have to wait. On Yext, it's almost instantaneous.

For example, if the client either changed an address, changed a phone number, needed to add a new service to the description, or didn't like a picture, etc., Yext updates it all in one place. So, with one quick update, we're done.

▶ **Content Development:** adding content to their blog, consistently.

We used to do it weekly. However, we found weekly was a little bit over the top. So now we do this once a month.

▶ **Link building:** building links and authority back to their website.

Reputation Management

We have just discussed the key elements that go into building a website that's going to convert with on-page optimization. A website that can rank well and build authority by building links and creating citations. However, without online reviews, oftentimes most of these strategies can fall flat.

Another important piece to the puzzle is having a reputation management platform in place to help your client's website get more online reviews.

The company will need reviews on Google, Yahoo!, Bing, and Citysearch. So, you want to bring something to the table that's going to help automate the way they get reviews from their real customers on a consistent basis.

Pay-Per-Click Management

The other thing that we do for most of our clients that come on board today is pay-per-click management.

For a long time, we were an SEO-only agency. We would optimize a client's website with proper on-page SEO, link building, and citation development. However, we found that occasionally there was a little bit of a control problem.

In the majority of cases, we would do everything we always do, and they'd get ranked, and it was high fives all around. However, occasionally, we would do the same thing in the same type of market for another client, and for whatever reason, it just did not rank, and they wouldn't get calls.

Of course, they'd be frustrated, and so were we.

However, when we started rolling out pay-per-click, we solved that problem. With pay-per-click, we are able to set up an AdWords campaign, bid on our keywords, and start ranking almost immediately.

We can create landing pages through Unbounce or a similar platform and start driving paid traffic and generating calls within the first couple of weeks. This begins to justify our services to the client and allows them to see a return on the investment they've made.

This piece is critical to your digital marketing toolbox in terms of the services that you bring to the table.

These days, we lead with our core offer of SEO and PPC. We do offer SEO-only. However, this is only for the rare occasions that the prospect doesn't want to do PPC, but SEO and PPC combined is ultimately the service we want them to buy because it gets them their ROI as quickly as possible.

For example, if the prospect says they don't want PPC and only want SEO, we do let them know that we have an SEO-only option but explain that the ROI may take months in that scenario. After we explain all of our services, our conversation would go something like, "After we begin work on your website, it's going to take probably six to nine months before the website starts to rank. This is because it takes about six to eight weeks to develop the site, write the content, optimize the titles, H1's and other SEO strategies, and get it up live for you. Then we've got to start to build some links and authority and depending upon how long your site's been up and how much competition there is, that could take about six to nine months. So, it might be six to nine months of investing in this service before you start to drive calls and leads."

Some people want that. Remember, that's what we always used to sell. I could still sell it today.

However, it's such an easier business model to say, "Hey, your best SEO strategy is for us to take care of all of your SEO work plus have a pay-per-click strategy in place. Yes, you're going to spend a little bit more, but it's going to generate calls and leads, as well as an ROI that's going to justify everything that we're doing."

Tracking and Measurement

Then, of course, tracking and measurement is an important part of your overall SEO strategy, as well. As you know, what you measure grows, so it's important to have a tracking system in place that will do this automatically for you. There are several software tools that can perform this service for you.

Basically, you need to be able to show your client a report each month or quarter that says, "Here's where you currently rank, here's what's happening with traffic, and here's how many calls you got." The proof is in the numbers.

Social Media Management

In some cases, our package also includes social media management. This is where we get admin access to their company's Facebook page, for example, and post on a consistent basis. There are several software tools that can help automate this process for you.

Overview

So, that's really our core service offering. We give them:

- ► A website that's built to convert
- ► On-page optimization
- ► Authority development on a consistent basis, which is going to help get the website and pages ranked in organic search
- ► Reputation process to get emails out to customers requesting reviews after the service call and drive new reviews on a monthly basis

▶ Pay-per-click management, in order to make sure they're showing up, getting traffic, and generating leads as soon as possible

▶ Tools to track and measure how many calls came in, key recordings of those calls, and truly quantify the return on investment

This comprehensive strategy right here has proven to be an extremely powerful service program to get our clients the results they are looking for.

It's the service model that works for us. You can choose to add to it, change it, or modify it as you see fit.

Now, that we have discussed our service model offerings, let's drill down on what it takes to get this kind of service model implemented.

Delivering the Service

In the following step, we'll cover what your out-of-pocket cost to fulfill this service model is and how much you need to charge to be profitable.

Creating the Website

When it comes to rolling out a website, we typically use WordPress. It's just an easy platform. It's very commonly used in the industry. WordPress has all kinds of themes and plug-ins, and it also tends to rank well on organic search.

We like working in WordPress, and it's worked well for us.

The other nice thing is there are lots of third-party programmers and developers that understand WordPress. So, if you don't do it in house and you don't have an internal team, you could find somebody on Upwork, or you could find a third-party company to build in WordPress for you.

There are some keys to making it work easily.

► **Use a Consistent Theme**

For WordPress, there are a lot of great themes out there.

The key thing I want you to do, though, is to get clarity on what theme you're going to use and try to be consistent with that theme.

For example, you don't want a problem if you select a theme, but the client prefers a different theme.

The theme that we build on today is FoundationPress. We do use a tool called Thrive Themes in certain areas, and in the past, I've used Genesis.

► **Follow a Framework**

You want to try and build your framework the way you build websites.

You should be able to identify where you are going to put the title, where you are going to put the video, and where you are going to put the call to action.

Then, once you can prove that it's an efficient method, the next step is to verify if it's also simplified enough to roll out something similar on a consistent basis. For example, the framework of the sites you create should have a similar look and feel, but not be so exact from client to client that it appears "cookie-cutter". It should also not be so basic of a template where they feel like they just got a manufactured template). Each website you create should follow a similar method of creation based on your proven framework.

► **Customer Header and Sidebar Graphics**

When it comes to the header and sidebar graphics, don't over-complicate it.

Ultimately, to roll out a home service for a local business website, all you need is at least 1 nice custom header graphic and 1 sidebar graphic.

You can use that same header graphic and sidebar graphic on just about every page, and it's just the content that changes along with whatever image you have within the content.

► Optimize the Content

Then, create well-written content about the service, such as, why someone should choose your client in that market.

As I stated earlier, optimize all of the pages for each of their services and each of the cities they operate in, along with the title tags and H1 tags. Also ensure that each page contains well-written and unique content, as well as strong calls to action.

This was something that has changed for us over the years. There was a long time where we could just use very similar content on our city pages for the clients. We did find that with each of Google's algorithm changes, it was safer to have unique content for each of the cities and each of the services.

We've always used unique content from one client to the next, but there was a time where we were using very similar content across a single client's service and city pages. For example, one client's Kendall page would have similar content to that same client's West Palm Beach page. Just to be on the safe side, I do recommend against that.

So, that's what we do from an on-page optimization perspective. You don't have to overthink it.

Next, let's discuss how to develop authority for your client's website.

Authority Development

The following are the key elements of authority development:

► Citations

With citations, we claim a lot of the listings manually, especially for the Google listing.

As we discussed, with Yext, we don't have to claim each and every one of them manually. I recommend using an automation tool like Yext, Local Site Submit, and/or BrightLocal that will do this for you. Today, we use a combination of these.

To break down the process, a client signs up, and then, we put them in Yext. After about 30 days, we pull a citation tracker report. On the report, we can see where there might be gaps in their rankings and/or their citations. Then we purchase a "citation burst", which provides a sudden influx from just a few citations to much more citations to increase your client's website authority.

Again, it just helps automate the directory claiming process which, in turn, helps to boost their ranking on Google Maps. This step in the citation building process is critical to your client's website success.

► Ongoing Blogging

For ongoing blogging, it doesn't need to be highly complicated to get this done effectively for your client on a consistent basis. For our service program, each client gets a blog a month.

The way to streamline this is to first come up with a list of about 25 topics at a time for your clients, and if you're niche-focused, which you will be, it makes it even easier. Then, order the content to be written through a third-party person or organization.

At this point, we use The Content Company. They're not the only content company out there that can write content for you. I happen to like them, but there are several services that can do this for you, such as, Textbroker, or Content Divas, for example.

The point is that, to fulfill on blogging, it doesn't have to be super complicated. The process can be as simple as: you come up with a specific topic, you order the content to be written, you review the received content, and then you copy and paste it onto their blog, and then it is done.

► Link Building

There can be some rare cases where your client may not be ranking well after implementing all of the SEO strategies I stated earlier. In these scenarios, link building may provide the little extra boost the website may need to move the needle.

One strategy that seems to work well is to drive the links back to your citations.

So, once you have your client on Yelp, Citysearch, Angie's List, Best of the Web, and similar sites that are being indexed, you can go and get some links to point back to those citations to gain them extra authority to their website. There are online tools that can help you with your competitive link acquisition, such as AHREF, SEMrush, or Raven Tools. To use any one of these tools, you first need to find your client's competitors online. Then enter each competitor's website address into AHREF, for example. It will then provide a list of links that this competitor has, and then have a virtual assistant work on obtaining these links.

As you do it, you're not looking to do hundreds of links. You're looking to find one or two quality links a month, and that's enough to have an impact. You just need a couple to the homepage, a couple to the service pages, and a couple to the city pages. Then, you should start to see some momentum on the ranking reports.

Reputation Management

Reviews are one of the most critical parts of your client's website presence. Good reviews not only help your client rank well on Google Maps, they also help with conversion.

We all know that before people choose to hire a company, they're looking at the company's online reviews. They want to see what other people who have dealt with this company are saying about their experience and whether they are legit. If they don't have any reviews, they are probably missing out on a lot of potential web traffic and phone calls. If they don't have a lot of reviews, that's not great either.

So, when you're reviewing a prospect's website, and you're painting the picture of what you're going to do for them, how you're going to help, reputation management is going to be a big piece of your overall SEO strategy.

In our business model, our clients are going out into the field and providing service. So, we use a tool, called Nearby Now.

It's an app that is installed on the technicians' phones, and as they go to wherever the job is, they "check-in" by clicking on a check-in button within the app. This action then grabs the coordinates of their location and passes that location to their website via a shortcode.

Then, to request the review, they type in the customer's name and cellphone number, and an email goes out to their customer that says something like, "Hi, thanks so much for choosing Tom Jones Plumbing. Would you please take a minute and write us a review?"

There's a lot of review management platforms on the market today, where after every service call, an email automatically gets sent to the customer thanking them and asking them to write a review. Local service clients need it as part of their SEO strategy.

This is one of those things you can include in your fee, and be able to say, "Look, we've got the best reputation management platform in the industry. We're going to help you implement it and we're also going to hold you accountable for it."

On the other hand, you can just pay that bill out of your pocket. Again, it's up to you.

The two reputation management tools that I've seen a lot of agencies use is Reputation Loop and BirdEye.

Reputation Loop is a popular local internet marketing space tool and they've got a white label platform.

The tool we use though is BirdEye. It's a more expensive platform, but it captures the client's reviews from across the internet and counts them all up, so we can then put a widget on their site to show how many reviews the client has in total.

We can automatically pull in their reviews from Google and Angie's List and Citysearch and have that on the reviews page of their website. Then, as they get each new review added, the client gets an automated alert.

Social Media Marketing

We do fewer social media marketing now than we once did. For plumbing companies, I have not found it to be just a slam dunk win for them.

With that said, they should definitely have an online social media presence with a created Facebook, Twitter, and LinkedIn profile, and they should be updated on a relatively consistent basis.

In a lot of cases, we can execute social media management for our clients without having to do a lot of extra work. We can use the same post for hundreds of plumbing companies in various markets.

They're not competing. It's pretty much irrelevant and there's no duplicate content as it relates to social media marketing.

Now, we post four times a week to each of our client's social media profiles and we queue it up in SocialPilot, just one of the many social media management tools out there.

We import each of our client's accounts, plug in our posts, and then schedule them throughout the week and the month. We book it out at least a month in advance.

If you're new to creating social media posts for clients, it's not as hard as it sounds. If you're niche-focused, you've got to write at least one post, and you can write that one post and have it used for 30, 40, 60, 100, 100-plus clients, and you're not doing it every day.

You or somebody on your team is sitting down once a week, plugging the posts into Hootsuite or SocialPilot, and pressing "publish." So, that's your social media strategy. It's not that complicated.

Pay-Per-Click Management

The other critical piece is pay-per-click management.

As I stated earlier, what we found to work best to get the campaigns started off quickly is to set up landing pages on Unbounce.

It's not a cheap platform, but it has a lot of flexibility. You could also use Thrive Themes or any other similar source for your pay-per-click management strategy.

After you select the tool you plan to use, this is the process you will follow:

► Create a simple landing page with good content where you can have a match to the keyword
► Set up a Google AdWords campaign and drive traffic to it
► Make sure you have your tracking in place

Overview

So, that's our service model, our SEO strategy, and how we implement our service program for our clients.

We've rolled out hundreds and hundreds of plumbing websites, using these proven strategies and this basic framework, in a very competitive vertical with some of the most competitive markets in the United States.

We claim the citations, put them on Yext, start blogging consistently, build some links back to their citation sources, do a couple of citation bursts, and make sure they're getting online reviews.

Probably more than 90% of our client base ranks on page one for many of their keywords. I can confidently say that following the above process is enough.

Many people who get stuck in any one or more of these areas may feel like there must be some secret SEO sauce that they need to go find, and they're out chasing it.

The fact is, if you get the right quality client, such as a truly reputable company that's legit, and then implement these basic strategies, you're going to get your clients the results they are looking for, and you're going to get your confidence, and your expert status. At this point, you'll have clients coming to you for help instead of you trying to find them, and that's when your business starts to grow exponentially. That's what we've been able to do with Plumbing & HVAC SEO and that's what I want for you and your niche business.

Pricing Your Offer

Now, that we've discussed how to develop your SEO strategy and how to implement it, let's discuss how to properly price your service offering.

In order to figure out how much your service should cost, we first need to take the following into account:

- ► Exactly what you are going to do for the client
- ► How much it costs you to deliver it

► What you need to charge on a monthly basis to deliver a healthy profit and still have the ability to grow and to scale

You have to create a list of all of the costs for the fundamental tasks you need to do for every new client.

A good way to do this is to create a basic spreadsheet that lists all of the elements. For example, you would list how much it costs to set up their website, how much it costs to get the content developed, etc.

When you plug this information in, you can be confident on what your setup cost is for a client, and what your monthly cost to fulfill for that client is.

Again, I'm going to walk through how this has worked for us. Your situation will not be the exact same, but it gives you a framework to work from.

COST ELEMENTS

First, it is important that you create a basic spreadsheet and in the first column, list all of the following services that you are going to offer for your clients. In the second column, list all of the costs that we will discuss, next.

Following are the key elements to take into account when completing your cost analysis. Each of these 12 categories will have its own separate line item in the cost analysis spreadsheet you are creating, based on the services you plan to provide:

1. Website and Graphics Design

You're going to need that header shot. You're going to need the internal graphics.

If you happen to be a graphic design artist or a web developer, you can do this yourself and you'll have very little cost associated. However, it will take up your personal time and energy.

If you're going to outsource, this could cost you about $1,000 or more. You're going to want to find a good quality developer and/or service that you can rely on to throw these projects over the fence and get them done, or develop an internal team, like we have.

We've got four graphic web developers in our web design development area. That's what they do all day. They set up our client's websites and they customize their graphics. Our hard cost is probably in that $850 to $1,000 per website range, even internally.

So, whether you outsource it or in-source it, the cost is probably going to be pretty similar unless you're doing it yourself.

2. Content Development

You need unique content for the "Home" page, "About Us" page, and "Our Services" page.

Again, this might be something you could do yourself if you happen to be a good writer and you don't mind putting in your time and energy, or you could outsource it to a content team.

The company we use is called, The Content Company. In the past, we've used Textbroker. Textbroker's content isn't quite as good, but it's an option.

Depending upon how many services they have and how many cities they operate in, you may be doing something between 15 and 25 pages at a time. So, figure out what your cost per page is to that provider, and then you can plug it in the spreadsheet, and you'll know exactly what your content's going to cost you to facilitate.

In some niches, you may find there are content companies that focus just on that niche. With niche-focused content companies, you can usually expect amazing content. Also, they will not only write your content, they'll also post it and do basic on-page optimization. I've heard of one in the dental niche that does this for $45 an article.

I haven't researched every content development service out there, but if you do a little research on your selected niche, you'll find there's several good companies to choose from.

3. Hosting

Of course, you'll need a hosting service where you're paying every month per each incremental client. Add this to your list of costs.

4. On-page Optimization

SEO setup I believe you should do in-house. That's title tags, H1 tags, meta descriptions, XML sitemap.

5. Citation Development

If you plan to do a citation burst for each client, it'll cost you a couple of hundred dollars. If you add them to Yext, depending upon how many clients you have, it should cost less than $50 per month. However, for a much greater volume of clients, it could cost upwards of $75 per month.

6. Blogging

I recommend at least one blog post per month. Again, you can either write your own content or use a niche-specific content company to write this for you.

7. Social Media Updates

You shouldn't have a hard cost for updating your client's social media posts unless you have a virtual assistant or somebody that's going to do this for you, consistently.

8. Link Building

Depending upon whether you buy links or whether you put that information through Web Ranker 2.0, make sure to list the cost for your selected link building service.

9. Reputation Management

If you use BirdEye or a similar reputation management company, it's going to cost you anywhere from $50 to $100 per month. Again, these costs depend upon where you're at in your business.

10. Call Tracking

You definitely need to allocate a cost for call tracking. CallRail, is the system we use for our call tracking at it costs about $2.10 a minute for us. However, there's a cost for that per-minute fee, which is hard to quantify, and it grows over time. So, just make sure you've allocated for this in your costs.

11. Welcome Basket

We always send a welcome basket to a client once they sign up, and it's a good practice for you to do in your business, as well. Once the client gives us their $1,500 credit card authorization, we like to commemorate this and have them look forward to our business relationship, so we send them a nice basket in the mail thanking them for choosing us. There are several upon several companies you can use for a welcome basket. For example, you can use a national company such as, Gourmet

Gift Baskets, or a very popular one such as, Harry & David, or you can even try to use a local gift shop. You can also get creative with this and send them any other kind of welcome gift that would be unique to your specific niche that they would find useful. There are all kinds of cool things you can send. Your welcome gift could be in the $50-75 range or less, depending on your budget, what you're planning to send, and how creative you can be.

12. Credit Card Processing Fees

Then you've got your credit card processing fees. Unless you're working with 100% liquid cash, make sure to include what your percentage fee is in your cost analysis spreadsheet.

Now, as you're looking over your spreadsheet, it's important to take some time to reflect on every single service you are going to provide and list each and every expected or estimated expense, including any that were not already mentioned above. As stated earlier, in the first column, type the items you are going to provide, and in the second column, enter in the cost for each item. Next, make sure you build in a 3rd column, as well, that tracks time frames such as costs per week, per month, and per year. Then, obtain your totals with a simple spreadsheet auto-calculation, and you now have the cost analysis for your services.

Now that you've decided what your services are going to comprise of and how much they are going to cost, let's look into setting the price(s) for your service(s). This way, you can control what your profits are going to be.

SETTING PRICES

Pricing is not only contingent on how much the services cost your business, but also how much you're comfortable charging.

What we've found to be comfortable is the following:

▶ SEO: $1,000 – $1,500 Per Month

We set up the website, write the content, do the on-page optimization, build the links.

Back when we first started, our SEO only offering was about $1,000 per month. That was our sweet spot. We felt comfortable with it and clients were buying it. We were growing residual income, and it worked well.

Our pricing has increased since then, but don't feel like you must charge what we charge. You might be in a niche where you can charge $5,000 a month. If you've got the confidence to do it, more power to you.

On the other hand, you might feel like, "I'm just getting started. I just want to get some proof underneath my belt. I want to land a couple of clients."

That's okay, too, but try to set your minimum at $750 per month.

At less than $750, you're going to feel like you're doing a lot of work and your momentum is going to grow very slowly.

▶ SEO + PPC: $2,000 – $2,500 Per Month

If you're going to do pay-per-click management in addition to SEO, then you could charge between $2,000 and $2,500 per month.

The costs are very controllable if you're doing the PPC yourself, can learn how to do this well, and can develop a little micro team to manage it for you.

If you're using an outsourced PPC provider, like InvisiblePPC for example, then there are going to be more tangible costs, so your price might have to be higher in that case.

► SEO + PPC + Social Media Management: $2,500 – $3,000 Per Month

If you are offering SEO and PPC, as well as social media management, then you should be charging between $2,500 and $3,000 per month.

What I find is that social media management is something that the client looking for SEO services usually wants or requests. It has a perceived value. It doesn't have a big impact, but in the age of social media, many clients expect this service and it has very little cost to you.

Once you have two or three clients, every additional client is an additional stream of profit. So, in some models, you might say, "Hey, for fractionally more, I'll include the social media as part of your solution," because you know it's something that doesn't have a tremendous cost to you.

► Online Marketing Complete Package: $3,000 – $5,000 Per Month

Then you might want to consider having an online marketing complete offer, such as SEO that includes: pay-per-click, social media, email marketing, retargeting configuration, and everything else that you want to include that will help move the needle for your client and have that be your higher-priced program.

What I'm trying to get you to do here is just think about what you are going to charge for these services.

For us today, our sweet spot is SEO plus pay-per-click. That means we're going to:

► Roll out a new website

► Develop pages for their cities and their services

► Optimize the website

► Optimize for conversion

► Update and claim their online directories

► Set up the Nearby Now check-in system and the review automation process

► Set up reputation monitoring and management

► Develop monthly blogging and link building

Then, in addition to that, we're going to manage their pay-per-click. Right now, these are our charges:

► For SEO only, we charge $1,590 per month

► For SEO plus pay-per-click, we charge $2,490 per month

► For our online marketing complete package, we charge $2,990 per month

Believe it or not, about 30% of our clients take our online marketing complete offering, even though that's not the main thing we try and push.

As I stated earlier, with our online marketing complete package, we offer SEO services which include pay-per-click management, social media management, email marketing (where we send an email blast once a month), and a retargeting service where they start to see their banner ads for everybody who visits their site.

TAKING ACTION

Now, what I want you to do is to develop no more than three core services, work out what they will cost you, and work out how you will price them. You don't want 20 programs and 100 different variations.

You want to be able to walk into your prospect's office or pick up the phone and tell your prospect in your niche, "Hey, I looked at your website. I checked out your online stuff. Here's what you've got wrong. Here's where I think we can improve. This is what we can bring to the table. These are our two options, this or this. Which do you prefer?"

That is much more palatable than, "Oh, let me come back to you with a proposal," or, "I could do this and that plus this a la carte, which adds up to this."

People like it when you just come in with one centralized service offering that makes a lot of sense to them.

Don't feel like you have to overthink every variation and every possibility. Come up with two or three core programs, "This is what I'm going to do. This is what I'm going to charge. We can get started tomorrow."

Once you have your 2 or 3 core offerings, then start meeting with people and you'll see your closing rate is a lot higher when you simplify what you're offering and make it something very clear.

Now that you've created your own spreadsheet detailing your costs, developed your service offerings and priced them out, you're ready to build your proposal to close the deal.

Presenting Your Offer

First, let's talk a little bit about how to present your services and the flow of the presentation process.

There are 4 important principles to consider when presenting your offer to your prospect:

1. Disclose Price Only After Value Shown

Price should only be discussed after the value has been shown, or the prospect's been disqualified.

What I mean by that is you shouldn't come in and say, "Hey, I'm excited about talking with you about how we're going to help you drive more leads and more sales," and they say, "How much does this cost?" "Well, we charge $2,500 per month," and then they'll say, "What? Forget it."

This happens when you haven't been able to build any value for them, first, before discussing the cost.

Therefore, we have developed a simple 4-step method to our Offer Presentation Process:

1. Identify the problem(s)
2. Show how the problem(s) directly impacts their profits
3. Solve the problem(s)
4. Then present the price for the solution(s)

If somebody reaches out to you or you've got an opportunity to chat with someone and they're just clearly a small operation, they're probably not going to be a good fit.

I want to encourage you to pre-disqualify people, but not in a disrespectful way.

You can spend hours with somebody, look at their website, show them the problem, show them the opportunity, but if they can't afford it and there's no way they could afford it, then you've just wasted your time.

At the beginning, wasting time's okay, but eventually, you're not going to have the time or energy to do a lot of those meetings when there's just no possible chance that they can afford to do it.

Maybe they shouldn't even do it. In a lot of cases, you might be able to convince that guy to do something, but long-term it's not going to be a good business fit. Not everybody is going to be right for you and your agency.

What I have found in the past is that they might say, "I'm really interested in what you guys do." Then, I'll say, "Great. Tell me a little bit about your company. How many trucks do you have? How much revenue?"

If they follow up with, "I'm just getting started," or, "We've got one truck," or, "I'm out there doing it," that's fine. I have no problem with that. I'm excited for them. However, I will jump straight to, "That's fantastic, man. I will tell you we're among the best in the industry, so we don't charge on the lower end of the price scale. Our programs range between $1,500 to $3,000 per month. I don't know if that's within the realm of reason for you or not."

At that point, if they say, "No, man. That's insane. That's more than my car payment right now," you can say, "Well, I appreciate your time. Maybe it's not going to be a fit right now." That way, you've saved yourself over an hour of going through the next 4 steps of our Offer Presentation Process.

However, if instead they say, "Hey, you know what? I understand and I'm still interested, even at that price point," then you take them through the rest of the process.

So, 99% of the time, you should not lead with price. However, if it's clearly unlikely to be a fit and you want to save yourself some time and energy, it's good to just lead with that question and get it out of the way.

2. Use A Live, Web-based Meeting

Most of your meetings should be done via live, web-based meetings, ideally where they can see your face and/or your screen. Join.me is great because it's free and it's very easy to use.

Almost everybody has a browser and can go to Join.me and enter a join code. So, that's what I recommend for most of you.

On a live, web-based meeting, you've got your screen up where they can see it. With your webcam on, they can even see your face and you're having a live business conversation.

An alternative would be Zoom.us, which I use for a lot of my meetings. I like Zoom but it may not be everyone's choice since there is a cost associated with it.

3. Create a Customized Program Overview

Next, you're going to create a customized program overview presentation so you can explain what you do for the client. For example, you'll say something like, "Here's the issues I found, here's the specifics of what we're going to do, here's how our services are going to solve the issues, here's how much it costs."

You're going to take the following presentation format, customize it for what you do, and then practice it on each call:

1. Ask your authority-building questions at the beginning
2. Go through your demonstration of where the issues are
3. Show your examples of how you've helped other companies
4. Explain what you're going to do to solve the issue(s)

These 4 steps should happen conversationally. It shouldn't happen with a long, monotonous, 19-point presentation.

I found a few people have taken me very literally with the presentation and have stated, "Man, I'm doing all these sales presentations, and nobody's buying."

So, I spend some time with them to drill down on where they're going wrong. I then experience their sales process, and we find what they're doing. They're going slide by slide on an actual PowerPoint-style presentation.

Real buying conversations don't usually happen on a PowerPoint slide type of format.

So, don't take me literally on this. Create a presentation process, but not an actual PowerPoint-style presentation. Then use the presentation process as a training tool, and go out and have a true, live, business conversation and let it flow naturally. As you're sitting at your desk in preparation for your meeting, take the time to role play and practice the conversation first for your initial five or six meetings. Get comfortable with it.

Now that you have the presentation down, let's talk about how you are going to close the deal.

4. Follow Up With A Proposal

You should have a document that outlines your program overview and an agreement that they can sign. That's how you close the deal. You get the agreement signed, you get the credit card authorization, and then you get to work.

In our case, we don't tend to get the sale right on that meeting. Probably eight out of 10 times, it's, "Great. Can you send me a document that explains this? That way, I have all the details." "Absolutely. We'll put that together for you."

Now, what you want to do is make sure that you close the meeting with a request for a follow-up, such as, "Fantastic. I'll put this together for you and have it in your inbox later today. Just so I know, what timeframe are you looking at to decide on this?... Okay, great. Can we schedule a time next week to sit down, go through the proposal and answer any questions that you might have?"

If you don't set that right then and there, you're going to be in chase mode. Chase mode is not ideal.

So, when say, "Yep, send me the information," then you send the proposal and agreement. Then, you must have a follow-up sequence in place. Our hot-lead follow-up is a series of emails that are going to automatically pursue that prospect after the sales presentation.

More than 80% of the time, they're not going to buy right on that first interaction, but they're interested.

So, you should be following up with them. You should be staying in touch, but you also want to use some automation to remain top of mind so that those opportunities don't go stale on you.

In the document, you've got the agreement and the terms and conditions. This is what they fill in with their name, contact information, and credit card details.

If you happen to be on-site, take that information down. If you're on the phone with them, have them send it back via scan and fax/email.

Once you've got the signed document in hand, you've got a new client and you're ready to get started working on their solution.

Conclusion

With this information figured out, you now know what you're going to sell to your prospects, how much it will cost you per client, how you are going to fulfill your services, how much it will cost your prospect to solve their issue(s), and how to present your offerings.

You now have everything you need to talk to prospects and close business. You can get things done and you can now start to scale.

In the next chapter, we're going to look at how you can properly scale your business form here and build your team.

 SEVEN FIGURE ACTION

Here are some actions that will enable you to implement the concepts we have covered in this chapter:

► Put together your service offering. Get clear on what you're going to do for your clients. Even if you are already established, it's a great time just to rethink, "Am I clear on what the best service offering is right now?"

► Figure out the cost elements and how you'll get the work done, as well as the steps to fulfilling, and who's going to do what.

► Establish your two to three offerings. Again, try not to have a huge list of options, but instead, drill down on just two or three main solution packages.

► Customize your program overview presentation, your proposal, and your client agreement.

Case Study: Setting up your service offering for scale

Jimmy Nicholas was the GKIC Marketer of the year a few years back. He sold his first website at just 17 and proceeded to build his agency to over $500K per year by the time he was in his early twenty's. The challenge was, his agency was built on a mix of project work, recurring revenue, multiple niches & a team of mostly friends. He was working 50+ hours per week and the profit just wasn't there. In 2013, after winning the GKIC Marketer of the Year Award, he got connected with Dr. Burleson, one of the top thought leaders/ trainers in the Orthodontic (Braces/Invisalign) Industry.

Jimmy ran a few marketing tests for Dr. Burleson's clients and got them great results. Jimmy decided to double down on Orthodontics & Dr. Burleson started referring him business. Today, Jimmy's agency, Jimmy Marketing, is the top marketing firm in the world for Orthodontists & has grown to over $3M per year with a completely virtual team.

You can listen to a full interview with Jimmy Nicholas
on how he built and grew his agency by going to

https://www.sevenfigureagency.com/jimmy-interview

6

DELIVER RESULTS 3: SCALE AND BUILD A TEAM

Set Up Your Business for Maximum Growth Potential

If you want to accelerate your agency to the next level as quickly as possible, you need to have a business that can scale.

If you're the person selling the clients and the only person doing the websites—if it's all you—you cannot scale and grow.

You can't sell, and do the work, and take care of clients all by yourself.

In the absence of a team, you can probably get to about $50,000 a month doing it all by yourself, but that's not true scale.

Now, if you're thinking, "Well, why do I need to grow any bigger or scale with a team?" Here are just a few of the benefits of having a business that has the ability to scale:

► You generate the **money** you need to live your desired lifestyle

► You have more **freedom** to choose how you spend your time

► You make a bigger **impact** by serving more clients

If you're building an agency that grows, you're building a team and you're pouring into their lives. You're helping your employees build a career path as they grow along with your business and you're also helping more businesses and more people find solutions.

Why Scale Matters

When you are trying to build an agency, often the first problem you seek to solve for is landing clients. You worry about how you get your clients and how you get them to pay.

Then, once you've got a couple of clients, you start to realize, "Man, there's a lot of things to do." And, in a lot of cases, there are just too many balls in the air to keep up with.

You've got to still have time to continue to market, to cold outreach, to produce webinars, to stay involved in your niche's association(s). Otherwise, while you are busy trying to keep up with the demand of providing service for your clients, you will stop having new clients coming in.

Each client that signs on needs to be served. You've got to get usernames and passwords, you've got to launch websites, you've got to write or obtain content, you've got to run pay-per-click campaigns, you've got to manage your communication with your client, and the list goes on. You have got to keep track of all the balls that are in the air.

What often happens is we start to get overwhelmed. I'm sure you've experienced this at some level. Whether you're just getting started or you've grown to a certain level, it can just feel overwhelming. It's like, "Oh my goodness. There's too much to do and not enough time, and I'm not making that much money anyway."

What can happen if you don't solve for this is you wind up with angry clients. Your clients start to say, "Hey, I didn't get the result," or, "Hey, I'm not hearing back from you," or, "Hey, you didn't do all the little things that I expected you to do."

Then, they cancel.

Further down the road, it can even lead to a bad reputation.

By now, I have really drilled that you should be in a very specific niche. One of the many reasons for this is that in a very specific niche, the good word about your business can spread very quickly. For example, when you get one client a great result, then they tell their friend, and so on and then, suddenly there's a little buzz in the niche that you're in.

If you can't figure out how to scale, you really can't grow beyond just being a freelancer, a one-man operation.

At the same time, though, if you do poorly, that word can spread quickly as well, and you can start to get a bad reputation just as quickly.

Getting some negative reviews can negatively impact your ability to grow.

Now, when the situation becomes overwhelming as you sell and fulfill all the services by yourself, you wind up having to make one of three possible choices:

First, what I often see happen the most, is that it's easy to get so busy trying to fulfill all the services by yourself and trying to keep all those balls moving in the air, that it becomes impossible to focus on sales and focus on landing new clients.

So, it's easy to just say, "Well, I guess, now that I've got some clients, I'm just going to invest 100% of my time in serving these clients and that's my job now."

Or, the alternative is, "Well, I'm just going to continue to sell them and hope that they stay. I'm just going to continue focusing on sales, and let the balls drop over on the fulfillment side if it must."

Neither of those options is a good one.

The third option, which is really the only successful one, is to create a team in place to help you fulfill you processes where you need help.

If you can't figure out how to scale, how to build a team, and how to put the right systems in place to get the work done while continuing to grow, then you really can't grow beyond being a freelancer or a one-man operation. You can't grow beyond working 50 to 80 hours per week.

On the flip side, if you can scale and build a team, it will allow you to proactively find new clients, serve them well, build rapport, and get this done consistently and well.

You can knock it out of the park and have happy clients and really retain them. Then, the good word can spread quickly, and you will have created the momentum and continued growth within your digital marketing agency that serves your lifestyle needs and provides for your financial freedom while helping other business succeed, as well.

Keys to Scaling a Seven Figure Agency

There are five keys to scaling your seven figure agency successfully when building your team. They are:

1. Make sure your model is built to scale
2. Map out your organizational chart
3. Find people who play at what you have to work at to accomplish
4. Develop the right systems and processes
5. Constantly be recruiting, training and managing

Before we look at these in detail, I want to spend a minute to define what it means to scale. It's a rather technical term.

If you look at an engineering drawing, you'll notice that engineers draw their structures to scale before any construction work actually begins. This allows for constructing a thorough building, ideally, without any of the structures breaking down during the process. Just like this building, if your business is properly scaled, it can be built to grow and flourish.

Now, if your business is not properly mapped out to scale beforehand, then as you continue to build and grow, different structures of your business can break down. This can lead to a business that can crumble to the ground like a building without a properly, pre-planned engineer drawing.

So, I want to unpack the five key principles to have your business scale without having different areas break down on you as you grow.

1. Make Sure Your Model is Built to Scale

We've talked a little about this in a previous chapter regarding the fundamental business model you want to put in place.

Most digital marketing agencies work with whatever kind of client they can get, instead of committing to work with only one very specific niche, as I mentioned earlier. Let's take a look for example, at a digital marketing agency whose client roster might consist of a roofer, a hair salon, and a dentist.

Then, this digital marketing agency does individual project work, because the roofer wants a new website, then the hair salon wants wants a new mobile app, and the dentist wants email marketing. This digital marketing agency wants to try to satisfy them all, with each of their different desires and for each of their different fields of expertise.

They don't have recurring revenue, so there's no consistency to what they're selling, how they're selling it or with the results they are getting.

The model painted here, which most digital marketing agencies try to accomplish, is built the opposite of scale. Again, instead of committing to one very specific niche, they are reinventing the wheel every time they get a new client. They are still trying to figure things out.

However, I don't want that for you. I want to make sure that your business is built to scale.

► That is why I need you to stop doing the project work
► That is why I need to stop dealing with the clients outside of your niche

There's no way you can scale if you don't commit to the right business model. So, here's a quick reminder of the scalable business model:

► **One niche.** The reason we have one niche is that we can serve that specific client. We can understand their keywords, we can map out a client launch process, we can put communication rituals in place that ultimately can be handed off to somebody else.

We can map out the system and the procedure for it and know this is how it's going to work every time, "We're going to do this to the website, we're going to claim these keywords, and we're going to put these directories in place, etc. This is what's going to happen in week one, this is what's going to happen in week four, and this is what's going to happen in week eight, etc." You can map this all out because it becomes very familiar territory.

If it's different every time, there's no way to map it out, to put a system or procedure in place, because every situation will be very different from the next. So, there is no way to scale in this method. However, with only one specific niche, you can figure all of this out.

► **Recurring revenue.** Recurring revenue means you have a client that is paying you a certain amount consistently over an extended period of time.

If you're doing project work, you're typically only getting paid once on the front end. Then, once the work is done on the project, you get the rest of the payment and the transaction stops.

I want you to have consistent, recurring revenue that's growing every single month and avoid project work. I also want you to be in one very specific niche, that way you've got a very consistent service offering that you do for a very familiar and consistent group of clients that you understand.

► **One program.** I want you to have a pre-thought-out program, not a custom-built one.

You want a productized version of what you do so that every client gets the same product offering. It might have a couple of different variations, but it's one product offering.

At the end of the day, you need to know, "This is the niche that I work in, this is how I get the clients, and this is the program that I implement for them without too many variations."

You know, "We're going to do the website, we're going to write the content, we're going to do the on-page optimization. This is what we're going to do on a monthly basis."

This is a model that's built to scale.

You have a productized offering that is the same for pretty much everybody that you serve, and you've got recurring revenue that comes in every single month.

This way you can reliably predict how much money you will have every month and you can start to put systems in place and teams in place to get the work done.

I can tell you, if you don't have this part right, if you don't have the model that's built to scale, you're going to have all kinds of issues. You can have the best systems, you can have the best procedures, you can have a cool organizational chart, etc., but you'll struggle if your model isn't built to scale.

2. Map Out Your Organizational Chart

Key two is to map out your organizational chart. I'm a big fan of the book, E-Myth Revisited, by Michael E. Gerber. If you haven't read it, this is kind of the masterclass on the concept of building a business. In the book, it describes how, if you must do it all yourself, then you don't have a business. You have a job.

> *The key is working out how to shift from doing it all yourself to having it done for you.*

So, the key is working out how to shift from doing it all yourself to having it done for you. You must build systems and procedures, and you must put a team in place.

In a moment, we're going to look more closely at what a proper organizational chart looks like for a digital marketing agency. However, let's first focus on the principles.

You've got to figure out who's responsible for what within your business. There are lots of different functions, such as sales, marketing, operations, account management, administration, IT support, etc.

What you want to do is identify who's responsible for all the different functions within your company and draw them out on a organization chart.

> *The fact is, in the early days, you probably do all or most of the functions within the company yourself.*

The thing that's going to set you free is the ability to see that organization chart as sits today, and where it needs to be in the next year and the next three years. Then, you need to strategically decide, "Here's where I'm at right now, all of these boxes, and here's what I'm going to change next."

I'm going to show you a process to help you figure out what the next two or three positions you need to fill within the company are to move away from the tasks that you don't like to do.

That way, you can do what you're best at, while putting people in place to do the remainder of the tasks.

3. Find People Who Play At What You Have To Work At To Accomplish

When we develop the organization chart, we must find people that play at what you must work at to accomplish.

Just realizing that there are people in this world who play at the tasks you don't enjoy doing can be a

---

This concept comes from one of my favorite books on this topic of business growth and systems and procedures, which is The Answer by John Assaraf.It's kind of a metaphysical book with daily rituals and affirmations, but there's a great section where he said the key thing that enabled him to scale his business and become successful—and he has all kinds of very, very successful businesses—was to find people who play at what you have to work at.

By that, I mean there are tasks in every business that we just don't enjoy doing.

For me, I don't love operations and I don't love doing flow charts and other similarly detailed tasks.

You'd think, as the owner of the business, I must do that. That's my responsibility. But for me, that's hard work.

But there are people for whom that's just what they love to do. They love to come in, and take all of the little pieces, and put them into a chart, and put accountability mechanisms in place, and follow through on every little thing.

In every aspect of your business, there are going to be things that you enjoy, are good at, are passionate about, that give you energy. There are also going to be things that you don't like to do, and that you're probably not very good at.

That awareness can be a gamechanger; just realizing that there are people in this world who play at the tasks you don't enjoy doing. For example, there are people who love to set up spreadsheets and run the numbers, who love to work on QuickBooks, and who love to keep the financials on track.

There are people who truly love to do the tasks you might just not enjoy doing. So, be aware that you need to find people who play and are passionate about the things that you must work at to accomplish.

We'll talk more about that in a moment.

4. Develop Systems and Processes

Now that you've mapped out your organization chart and started to realize that there are people out there who play at what you have to work at to accomplish, the next thing you have to do is to start to map out your systems and procedures, at least at a basic level.

Ideally, these are the things that you do today and that should be done, in the perfect world, every single time.

You need some systems and procedures put in place for each of the tasks you don't enjoy doing so that you can hand it off to somebody in each area of the company who is passionate in each of these tasks. That way, the right person can step in, understand what needs to be done, do the work for you and do it well.

Now, there's a shortcut here, that I'd like to share with you. If you find a good project manager who specializes in systems and procedures, you can even have them build the systems and procedures for you.

That'll let you focus on what you do best if you don't happen to be great at systems and procedures, and or just don't enjoy this part of the process.

5. Constantly Be Recruiting, Training and Managing

Finally, as it comes to scaling your business, you must constantly be recruiting, training and managing.

You must constantly say, "Okay, these are the positions I need to fill." Always be on the lookout for good talent that you can bring into your company.

As entrepreneurs, that's one of our key functions in our business: to recruit good talent. We train and develop, put systems in place to help the people understand their job, and then strive to keep them motivated and engaged.

This way, your employees know what their expectations are and what they're supposed to get done on a consistent basis, and you can hold them accountable to do their work.

As you start to get to the place where you can afford to go hire your operations manager or your account manager, the next questions are:

- ► What does the recruiting process look like?
- ► What kind of ad should you put?
- ► What kind of interview questions should you ask?
- ► How can you make sure that you get the right people within the company?
- ► What should you pay for those types of roles?
- ► Then, how do you manage that?

As you grow and as the entrepreneur, after doing everything yourself, to now having a team in place, the next questions are:

- ► How can you manage quality?
- ► How can you keep the team members engaged?
- ► How can you make sure that they're doing a good job and they're meeting expectations across the spectrum of the organization?

This is all mission-critical. These are the key things that are really going to help you scale, and help you grow.

Putting It Into Practice

To put these concepts to work in your business, the first thing I want you to do is to map out your organization chart.

By that, I mean what are the roles within your agency? Who does what? Who's responsible for what?

As I mentioned earlier, I'm a big fan of The E-Myth Revisited, by Michael Gerber and I also like the following two books by Gino Wickman, Traction: Get a Grip on Your Business and The EOS Entrepreneur Operating System.

I believe the true implementation piece of this whole concept of systems and team building really is powered by an Entrepreneur Operating System.

Any digital marketing agency, operating at less than $10 million per year in revenue, really stands to learn a lot from the Entrepreneur Operating System.

Here's an example of how the Entrepreneur Operating System lays it out.

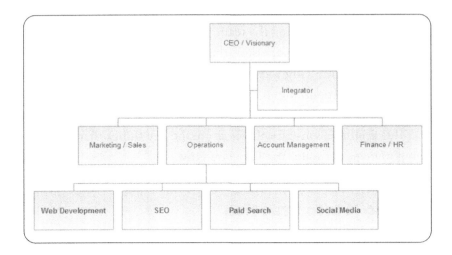

At the top, you've got a visionary, and then you've got an integrator, who directly reports to the visionary.

▶ The **visionary** is responsible for questions like "What's the business? What are the products? What are the services we offer to our clients? What's the vision of the company? Where are we going as an organization? What are the goals? What are the targets?"

That's what the visionary does. Usually, as the owner, you're going to be the visionary.

▶ The **integrator** is the person who takes the vision, all of those big ideas, all of those big concepts, and puts them into play, and determines if a new process is a good idea that the company should implement or if it's probably a little bit outside the realm."

They kind of hold the visionary to reality. The integrator will basically speak in terms of, "These are the resources we have; these are the constraints, this is what we can get done, and this is what we can't get done because of xyz."

The integrator is almost like a chief operating officer and is responsible for putting the systems in place, communicating across the department underneath, and making sure that the things that need to get done actually get done.

Depending upon where you're at in your agency, whether you have a business partner or not, you're probably doing both.

You're coming up with the vision, and you're trying to make sure that everything gets done.

I can tell you that you're going to move a lot faster when you get a high follow-through person underneath you that can help execute that type of stuff.

If you don't have an integrator yet, that might be somebody who can be handy for you. If you do, then obviously you are well on your way.

Below the visionary and the integrator, are all the functions within the company, such as:

▶ Marketing: how do we generate leads and awareness in our marketplace?

▶ Sales: once a lead comes in, how do we convert it into a signed deal?

▶ Account management: handling the relationship, communication, and monthly reporting with the client, as well as retaining the client base.

▶ Operations: completing the services promised to the client base.

▶ HR/Finance: handling the bills and handling employee paperwork and benefits

Next, you can see in the chart that we've got website design, SEO, pay-per-click management, and social media.

What I want you to do is to create a chart like that for yourself. A good tool to use is Smart Draw.

I want you to go in and put your name on all the boxes that you're currently in. This will be an eye-opener for you because you might realize you are doing a lot of heavy lifting by yourself which is causing you to feel burned out. You probably feel like you have 100 balls in the air and it's because you do.

To be able to scale and grow, you must realize you can't do it all yourself and that you must put some people in place to work efficiently.

As stated earlier, you must get people who can step into certain roles within the company you don't enjoy doing. That's what's going to free you up to grow and scale. This is going to be an extremely powerful process to help bring some light to the issue(s) you may have within your business.

As you go through this process, highlight the roles you are doing that are taking the most time and energy.

You can mark in green the things that are taking a lot of energy out of you, and then in orange the things that are maybe problematic. Maybe you have somebody in place who isn't doing a great job and who needs to be reworked, for example.

Once you highlight in green the roles you know you shouldn't continue to do because they are taking the most time and energy and you don't enjoy doing them, those will be the positions you need to replace next. These are the roles that you need to avoid doing yourself and hire for.

When I first did this, it was my business partner Dean and me sitting in an office and it was Josh, Dean, Josh, Josh, Josh, Dean, Dean, Dean. At the beginning of our business, the two of us were doing everything. However, we quickly learned which roles we needed to replace next.

For us, we realized we needed to put somebody in place to handle the operations so that every time we get a new client, their website gets built, their on-page optimization gets done, and their citations get ordered, consistently.

Then, we realized we needed to put somebody in place to handle the clients for the ongoing monthly communication. This way, when the client calls saying, "Hey, what is the status on this? What about that? How is this doing?" they have someone who's dedicated to serving and supporting them to retain the client relationship.

When you have somebody who's handling the operations, and you have somebody who's handling the client relationships, it frees you up to go out and focus on continuing to sell, continuing to get new clients, and continuing to grow your digital marketing agency.

This is a powerful exercise that I strongly recommend that you do quickly.

Again, as you do this, you want to focus on finding people who play at what you must work at to accomplish.

If operations and website design is work for you, there are people you can hire who have a passion for making websites and love doing on-page optimization.

If selling and creating video content is work for you, there are people you can hire who have studied in this area, practiced at it, and enjoy this part of the business.

Don't feel like just because you're not the sales savvy guy that this means you don't have the opportunity to put a good business model in place that can truly scale.

When I work on this with my Seven Figure Agency clients, I drill down in a lot more detail. I carry out an Activity Inventory to not only help you identify how you are spending your time, but also to categorize it in levels of competencies, such as: genius, excellence, competence, and incompetence.

That way, we can work out exactly what you should be focusing on and where you need to get help.

For now, I just want you to spend a little bit of time thinking about where most of your energy is being invested.

Once you're aware of how your spending your time in your business, you might start to say, "Oh my goodness, I'm spending so much time doing this stuff that I'm terrible at." That's fine, you can adjust. You can figure out ways to move out of those tasks. Awareness precedes change. That's why we do this essential activity.

Your Next Two Hires

Now that you've determined the roles that you need to hire based on the tasks you don't enjoy doing and time efficiency, your next focus is going to be on hiring the next two to three positions on your organizational chart that you can push yourself away from.

Where can you say, "Okay, I can separate myself from this particular area in the company, ASAP, which will free me to do the roles which I'm best at performing."

This is the start of your business growth scale plan. You've now got your organization chart in place as it sits today, you know your next steps, and you know what your organization chart should look like after your first couple of hires.

When you've spent some time internalizing what roles you enjoy doing and which you are best at performing, you're ready to try and find people who can play at what you have to work at to accomplish.

Those are the next two to three positions to hire for in your business. I want you to get that dialed in quickly so you can start looking in your marketplace for those individuals who would fit nicely into the specific areas that you need, and the roles that are going to be critical to your agency's success.

 **SEVEN FIGURE ACTION**

► Design your own current organizational chart, as outlined in this chapter

► Identify how you are going to find people who play at what you work at to accomplish

► Identify the profile and responsibilities of your first/next two hires

Case Study: Delivering Results

Michael King spent over 10 years working with his brother to build his LASIK business from one clinic to over 7 locations. His unique experience in developing the business from the ground up gives him expert insight in the field—specifically working with Ophthalmologists who specialize in LASIK procedures. It was an easy transition for him to grow from managing one group to diving into digital marketing management for multiple providers.

After realizing digital media was his greatest asset and launching his marketing agency, Michael knew that getting his clients great results was the most important driver for his long-term success. Because LASIK is a procedure that can only be done once, Ophthalmologists are constantly looking for new clients.

He decided to focus on not just generating leads and providing a great service, but also helping his clients convert the leads he generates to sales.

It is extremely important to understand your niche and how to best develop your client's marketing to convert leads. For Michael's niche, he found that it was highly important to drive the client through his funnels by optimizing pricing on a client's website.

Michel has since grown to over $50K in monthly recurring and only getting started! He is well on his way to becoming a seven figure agency.

You can listen to a full interview with Michael King on how he built and grew his agency by going to

https://www.sevenfigureagency.com/michael-interview

PART THREE

RETAIN CLIENTS

7

RETAIN CLIENTS 1: STRONG KICKOFF

Getting Client Relationships Off to a Strong Start

O ne of the most important factors in growing a seven figure agency is being able to keep your clients so satisfied that they stay with you long-term.

In the first two parts of this book, we've focused on the steps you need to go through to attract your ideal clients and the best-in-class methods to follow to structure your business to serve your clients well.

You've focused on choosing the right niche and positioning yourself as the expert and as the go-to company in the niche that you've selected.

You also now have all the tools and resources to put a strategic marketing strategy in place to get the customers coming to you, looking to you as the leader in your niche industry, and paying a premium price for your top-level service. You now know how to fulfill the services you offer and can feel confident that you can get the work done and get your clients results.

However, it doesn't make sense to invest a ton of time and a ton of energy on trying to get get clients if you can't retain them. So next, we will focus our attention on how to retain clients long-term.

If you can't retain your clients long-term, you'll be losing almost as many clients as you bring in to your business. You're going to be like a mouse on a treadmill, constantly taking one step forward and one step back.

Simply having a sales focus or even a service focus isn't going to get you where you want to go.

It will get you some clients, but unless you execute well and unless you've thought through how you're going to fulfill and how you're going to provide a world-class experience to your clients, you're not going to be keeping these clients long-term.

In this part of the book, we focus on helping you establish the fundamentals from an account management perspective so that you can retain as large a percentage of your clients as possible.

So, this part of the book is really about customer retention, because retention is critical.

From our experience, there are three key elements to this:

- ▶ Strong Kick-Off
- ▶ Communication Rhythm
- ▶ Seed the Vision

We'll look at each of them in more detail, starting with the importance of having a strong kickoff.

Starting with a Great Experience

One of the things we did early on was to make sure we created a positive customer experience right out of the gates. Do this and your customers will stay longer. Don't do it and you might see some cancellations in the first few months.

The key things we have introduced are:

► Client setup sheet
► New client launch call
► Welcome sequence

Let's look at each individually.

Client Setup Sheet

One of the things we've crafted within our business to ensure a great customer experience right from the start is the client setup sheet.

This makes it easy to collect the information you need to get started as quickly and easily as possible. This includes the important information we're going to need such as their usernames, passwords and main keywords.

It seems very simple, but it genuinely does help us get started very quickly and also comes across as professional. It shows that we are serious about what we are going to do.

New Client Launch Call

Then we have a new client launch call. This call is pretty detailed. We don't just say, "Hey, thanks for signing up. We'll be in touch with you in 30 days once your website is ready."

It's an in-depth consultative conversation where we collect essential information, but also reconnect with the client to discuss their goals and what they're hoping to accomplish in this relationship.

We also find out what else they're doing as a company to market themselves. We learn about what their unique selling proposition is and how they position themselves in the marketplace.

Having a good 30-minute to 90-minute structured conversation consummates the relationship. This launch call makes them feel like, "I made an investment and there's somebody real on the other side of this business who is taking the time to understand my business and who understands where I'm going."

Dean and I don't orchestrate these launch calls anymore. We have account managers we've trained as well as a team in place to handle each launch call and nurture the relationship with each client.

Have confidence that you will eventually be able to manage yourself out of the process. We've done this, and you can, too.

There was a time I never thought that would be a possibility, because I'm on our videos and I'm the guy who wrote the book, and I'm the face of the company. So, you'd think clients would only want to deal with me, personally.

We found that the longer the launch call goes, the deeper the relationship is right out of the gates.

However, we've found that if you've got a structured process in place, clients are just as happy to work with an account manager at your business.

Now, let's continue diving into our launch call process. Another series of questions we ask our clients on our launch call is, "What's the best number to reach you at", "What email address do you want on the website?" and "What services do you want to focus on?"

This step will be powerful in positioning you in your client's eyes as the expert.

Now, the length of each launch call can vary from 30-90 minutes, because the launch call flow depends partly on the available time frame the client has and on the flow of the conversation. There are clients who only have 30 minutes that they can set aside for the launch call. So, in these cases, the account manager can go through the call in a short, quick and to the point method to gather the information, check the boxes, and then proceed to follow up on all of the action items after the call. However, we have found that most clients have the time for about an hour or so for the launch call and so the account managers are able to be very thorough and conversational on the call. Just like the sales conversations, the flow of the launch call should match the flow of the conversation with the client during the information gathering process.

In addition to having the account manager on the launch call, we have the writer who is working on their website projects join in on the call, too.

We try to pull as much information from the client as possible to get a true feeling of what their business is and of the passion they have for their own business so we can put it into the content as well as translate it into the look and feel of the website.

We found that the longer the launch call goes (of course, within reason!), the deeper the relationship is right out of the gates and ultimately the better, and more long-term relationship we have with the client.

Welcome Sequence

The next key element you want to have is a welcome sequence, which is something that we didn't have when we were starting out.

We were getting a few clients and we hadn't thought any of this stuff out.

We would get a new client and we would send an email, "Hey, please send me your domain and your hosting access," and that was it.

Then, to the perception of the client, we would just kind of disappear for a while with no other communication in place and we had clients who would disappear on us relatively, shortly thereafter.

We gradually created our current launch call process and our launch call setup sheet, but really what I think had the biggest impact was the welcome sequence.

I state this because the more you can communicate with your client on the front end, right after they sign up, the better the probability that your client really buys into the program they've signed up for long-term. Your client will realize, "Wow, I'm with the right company, they are very thorough, they know what they are doing, and I'm going to trust in their process."

In addition to our welcome sequence, we send them a welcome basket as well as a welcome kit in the mail and then we also have a sequence of emails powered through Infusionsoft.

For the welcome basket, we invest about $75 through Gourmet Gift Baskets to simply say, "Welcome aboard, we're excited to have you."

For the welcome kit, we send them a custom printed binder, which includes our testimonials, an overview of our program, a timeline of what to expect, and a copy of our book. The welcome kit is a separate mailing.

Another touch that we have is a handwritten note, directly from the sales representative that signed them up, or from the owner, saying, "Thanks so much for your business, we're excited about working with you and helping you take your company to the next level."

All these ideas have just come along the way from different situations we've been in, ourselves.

We used to be in a coaching program and got an idea that we should put something in their hands. It's just so impressive when you sign up for something online and then get something physical back in the mail.

Very few people are doing this today. It's one of those special touches that's been lost. In my own personal experience, every time I buy something and then someone sends me something I can hold, it changes my whole outlook of the company.

A few years back, Dean and I joined a mastermind, where we spent a lot of money on it and we had very high expectations for it. However, we didn't even get anything in the mail. Not even a thank you card with a 25-cent stamp.

Then we recently joined Strategic Coach where the experience has just been phenomenal. Before we went to our first meeting, we received a handwritten thank you card and a little USB adapter with an audio program on it.

The feeling we got when we went there was, "We're with a first-class organization." As an SEO company, you have such an advantage because hardly anyone is doing this.

Our binder started with us running over to Office Depot when we were signing three clients a month and printing out a color sheet and putting it in the plastic slot in the front and putting our papers in the middle and sending it out.

That has morphed into us getting them professionally printed and buying them at a bulk rate of 50 at a time, which is so much cheaper than buying them individually at Office Depot.

When they got it in their hand, one of our clients said, "I got your binder in the mail, I know I'm with the right company."

In the welcome emails, they get about 60 to 90 days' worth of emails dripped out over a weekly basis.

Some of them come from me, some of them come from their account manager, some of them come from the customer service manager.

In addition to the live communication and the real emails that come from their account manager, it helps them feel pursued and like we are constantly reaching out and requesting additional information and letting them know what's going on in their program and in their website.

In that launch sequence, they're being indoctrinated on the front end. Some of the things it includes are:

► Welcome to Plumber SEO, you made the right decision, we're excited about working with you.

► Here's a video explaining what you're getting over the next 90 days.

► Here's your account manager.

► Here's what our office looks like, it lets you meet our team.

I highly encourage you to create a sequence like this even for your early-on clients. The more you are reaching out to them with automatic communication in addition to real communication, the more they feel like they're getting a world-class experience, the higher probability that they're going to stay during the initial phase and stay long-term.

Why Sending Things in the Mail Matters

Make sure that you prioritize sending your clients things in the mail. It is something real and tangible and comes in a FedEx package, or an envelope. And most importantly they get something in their hands.

This is especially important as you get more and more national.

You're getting better positioned in your niche, and you've got clients now who are not in your backyard but may be five, six, seven states away.

You may never meet in person and all they've got from you is your book, your downloadable guide, and at least a couple of conversations on the phone.

We're in a business that is strictly digital and there's so few companies in the SEO industry that do this.

You want to provide them with physical stuff in the mail.

You're going to want to do that yourself on the front end. As you start to get more clients and you have more financial resources, you might want to have an executive assistant or somebody in the office where that's something they do. When a new client comes in, Infusionsoft sends them a task to write a handwritten note on behalf of the sales representative. Don't use Send Out Cards for that touch. If it's not handwritten and hand addressed, it loses that feel of being a real handwritten note.

So that's the onboarding process of a client. We found that when we introduced those three steps, such as the launch call, the new client setup sheet and the email and mailing sequences, our retention rate improved significantly.

It's all about mass communication on the front end. It gives you an advantage because remember, we're in a business that is strictly digital and there's so few companies in the SEO industry that do this.

None of the big guys do it and most of the small ones don't. Many of the small SEO companies just "set it and forget it" or they have an online form and that's their main communication method. However, for us, we're always trying to be as hands-on as possible.

Sometimes it's just the little things that cost you only a few dollars but can cement the relationship with your client.

We're always thinking of new things that we can do or new programs we can develop to add value to our clients and that we can put in their hands.

We are currently updating our welcome binder and putting it into a box with a lot of other things, so that when they sign up, they get a big box full of goodies from us.

We are always thinking of something you can put in the customer's hand every month or at least once a quarter.

It may be just a little knick-knack. We have sent out a little knapsack with a funny thing on it for our plumbers. We have also sent out coffee mugs.

We once sent one of our great customers, who has been with us now for three years, a coffee mug with our logo on it and she called us and said, "Hey thanks so much for the mug, I was having a really bad day and then I walked in and saw a box on my desk, I opened it up and it was your coffee mug with your logo and a little $10 Starbucks card, and it really made my day."

At the same time, another customer that we signed up, brand new, said, "I just got your mug, that's great. It was a nice touch, thank you very much." So, it's those little things that don't cost you much that no one else is doing that will give you such an advantage, so be creative.

Now remember, of course you must also be able to fulfill on good service, that's expected. However, once you have the service fulfillment part down, little surprises and special touches like this can go a very long way for your clients.

 SEVEN FIGURE ACTIONS

Have a look at how you can apply this in your own agency by developing your:

- ► **Client setup sheet**
- ► **New client launch call**
- ► **Welcome sequence**

Each of these 3 items will not be perfect when you get started. Just get going with a rough draft in each category and improve them along as you go.

8

RETAIN CLIENTS 2: COMMUNICATION RHYTHM

Building Relationships That Make Clients Stay

While the initial impression is important and sets the tone for the future relationship, keeping clients long-term requires a consistent and effective communication rhythm.

As we discussed, since your clients are paying you a significant fee of perhaps $1,500 to $2,500 per month, it is imperative to have a great setup for your "welcome" communication that is both fun and interesting for your new clients as they come onboard.

During the first few months, each of your new clients is receiving a welcome package in the mail, getting their new website built, receiving updates on directories claimed and updates on social media profiles, etc. You have now built all of these consistent touch points for your clients, and during the early days, these actions will carry the momentum for you, to the point where they're hopefully quite happy and excited for the first three months.

By month two or three, they may not have yet received a call from a prospect based on your efforts, and they may not have seen any true result, since the SEO process takes time. However, based on what you've shown them and based on the communication level you have established, they believe that it's going to work out well. There's an excitement level there.

However, right about that 90-day to 120-day mark, that's where the rubber starts to meet the road and they're starting to think, "Okay, now I need to start to see some return on this investment."

Assuming you've done a good job, it's really in month three and four that you're going to start to see them get more calls, get ranked higher, and get more traffic to their site. However, it's at this point where you must switch it up for your client and create an ongoing customer communication process that goes beyond month three.

You can't just let that initial blast carry you through and expect the client to stay with you for two years, three years, or even five years.

You must earn that relationship on a monthly basis.

Earning that relationship takes a focused and strategic effort. You must know what you're going to do and what you're going to say every single month to your client base, consistently, otherwise it simply won't happen.

Let me share with you how we realized just how important this is and what we put in place to create a powerful communication rhythm.

How We Discovered the Importance of Communication

During our first two years in the business, it was just my partner Dean and me, and then early on, we hired one operations guy.

What we were doing was, selling, selling, selling, then working hard to get the work done and to get our clients the results they were looking to get.

That didn't leave a lot of time to talk to the customers, build rapport, and be in consistent communication with them.

We were kind of hoping that, if the results were there, they were going to stay with us, and things would be fine and dandy.

However, the truth is that we had a little bit of a retention issue. So, we learned some things along the way, and we want to share those with you so that you don't have the same retention issues and you can keep the highest possible number of clients in your digital marketing agency for as long as possible.

We first found that we must put in place the proactive client onboarding process that we have already discussed in the previous chapter.

Then, we also learned that we needed a process to maintain the momentum that we had already established.

You need to have a proactive strategy for communicating with your customer.

So, you need to have a proactive strategy for communicating with your clients and circling back with them and letting them understand what you're doing and what you're up to.As part of this communication strategy, you must have periodic calls set up on a consistent basis where you're reviewing their progress, reviewing the KPIs and discussing the next steps with your client.

Of course, in addition to that, you must get them results. If you create the mission of your business to help your clients increase their sales and grow their business, it seems reasonable to think they should stay with you.

This should be the foundation of what you're trying to accomplish within your business. Everything you do, from how you set up their website, to how you claim the directories, to how you help them get inbound leads, is all about growth.

If you can consistently get clients a return on their investment, you might feel they should stay with you. I mean if they're spending $1,500 or $2,500 a month, but they're getting $5,000 or $6,000 in profitability, you might think there would be no reason for them to discontinue their service with your agency.

The harsh reality is that good results alone aren't enough. There are many reasons why someone might decide to move on. So, you must take steps to minimize the risk of that happening.

Great results alone don't ensure retention and that's an unfortunate lesson that we had to learn.

It's not just about getting the results, it's not just about getting on page one, there's more to it than that.

One of the most effective steps you can take is to establish a rigorous monthly review process.

Monthly Review Process

To establish this process, I recommend that you focus on getting a monthly review call scheduled with each of your clients. That should be a real call, whether it's a phone meeting or web meeting.

If your office is physically close to a client's location, you might want to do these calls live in their office or yours. We haven't done this for at least three years, and if I gained a new client in South Florida, I wouldn't meet with them in person. Instead, I would let them know, "Yeah, you can swing by our office or we can get on a web meeting and speak live."

However, by going out to their office and spending time driving around town, you stifle your ability to grow if you've got to meet with every client face to face.

So, a live call, via phone or web meeting is ideal.

Next, you'll need to have a structured ritual to what that call is about.

Every month there's got to be something new that you and your team are working on. In the beginning, it's setting up the website and creating the content and claiming the directories.

When you get into month four and month five, it might be some new links that you guys were able to develop, it might be some new keywords that emerged on page one.

It's about being able to communicate what you've been working on and the results that have been achieved.

As I stated earlier, we use BrightLocal to look at the ranking reports and see how they're moving up in rank. Maybe we pull up a couple of search results, "Hey look, here's where you are now ranking for Mississauga emergency plumber, Mississauga drain cleaning, isn't that cool?"

We can also show them what's happening within Google Analytics by pulling up a live Google Analytics window and showing them a three month, or a six-month, or a nine-month chart, and by showing how that number has increased.

We can also go through the call volume numbers. Ideally, you're using CallRail or a similar call tracking system so that you can show them, "Look, not only have your rankings and analytics improved, but you've also got an increase in calls from people going to your site." You can let them see, for example, that they got 27 or 87 or 112 phone calls directly via the web.

Showing your clients this type of traction gets them excited about what you're doing and proves that what you're doing is working for them and that there's momentum. This is an important part of keeping them informed as well as involved in the process and makes them more likely to stay.

However, the process itself is not enough. It's not enough to impress them with what you've done. There is another important element that we'll dive into in the next chapter.

Why Clients Leave

One of the most important lessons we learned in the early days was the biggest reason why a client will leave.

You may think the number one reason they leave is because they're not getting results, but the number one reason a client leaves is because of perceived indifference.

As well as getting clients results, you must make them feel pursued and appreciated.

If the customer doesn't feel like you are there for them, like you care about their business or like you're working hard to earn whatever it is that they're paying you on a monthly basis, then they're probably going to end up canceling.

That will happen even if you're getting them great results, even if they're getting a lot of calls.

That's why you must make sure that, as well as getting them the results, you must make them feel pursued and make them feel appreciated.

I know that sounds a little bit sentimental and almost like a romantic relationship, but these types of client relationships where the client is paying you a reasonable sum, between $1,500 and $2,500 per month, you can't just "set it and forget it".

You must be continuously working on the relationship. You can leverage technology, emails, and direct mail to an extent, but you can't hide behind the technology. As we discussed, you need to have live phone calls where you're talking to the customer about their business and their goals.

These live phone calls, however, are not going to be randomly made. You will need to develop an ongoing program of communication so that your clients feel you are delivering for them.

That's how you can develop the relationship, where they're not only getting results, but they also feel connected to your business and they know that you care about them. This is one of the key components to getting your clients to stay with you long-term.

Also, keep in mind that every morning your client gets up, whether they're getting amazing results or subpar results, they're trying to think of ways that they can cut back and save money. One of the ways they can do that is by canceling your service. So, you need to be proactive and have a communication plan in place. We'll dive into how to best do this in the following chapter.

 SEVEN FIGURE ACTIONS

To take advantage of what you have learned in this chapter, set up your own monthly call process with a clear agenda for each call.

9

RETAIN CLIENTS 3:
SEED THE VISION

Inspire Your Clients About What Happens Next

While talking to clients about what you've done is important, it's not enough to make them stay.

You need to make them see that you are thinking about their future and looking for ways to make things better for them.

That means you must gradually shift away from recapping what happened in the past to start talking about what you're going to do over the next 30, 60, and 90 days.

The fact is, talking about the past will only get you so far. So, after you've recapped the results, you want to talk about what's coming next.

This conversation is driven around questions like these:

- ► Are you planning any upcoming seasonal promotions?
- ► What services should we shift to promote more due to the change in season?
- ► Are you planning to offer any new or additional services?
- ► Are there any upcoming events to promote?
- ► Are there any special products or services we can feature on the blog or the social media profiles?

You also need to state what homework you need them to do. One of the best things you can do in the ongoing communication is to give them work that will include them in the process, as well.

For example, you may need them to:

- ► Be more proactive about requesting reviews
- ► Take some additional photos of their team or photos of the jobs that they're completing
- ► Provide any updated coupons or specials for the website

You should always have at least one or two nuggets that you could say, "Here's what we've been able to accomplish already, here's your latest rankings, and here's what we're currently working on, isn't this exciting? Now here's what we need from you."

Then on the following month's conversation, you should circle back with them regarding any pending items. On this call, you might say, "Hey, what's the progress on this? I never got those pictures," or "I noticed you guys haven't been checking in."

That way you're almost coaching them as a client on what they need to do to ensure that it's a collaborative process.

Communicate the Future

As I stated earlier, you need to communicate what you're going to be working on over the next 30 to 90 days.

Plant the vision for them. For example, you might say, "Over the next 90 days we're going to be updating the blog and we're going to place an additional emphasis on those two or three main services that you're more interested in along with those two keywords you'd like to see improved."

If you take this type of approach to the monthly review call with the client, you re-anchor the relationship.

Now that we've discussed the "meat and potatoes" of the call, let's talking about how each call should begin. At the beginning of each monthly call, there should be a conversation starter, such as, "How's business going?" or "How are you tracking towards your goals?"

You should have a little bit of rapport time at the beginning of the conversation before diving into the results.

However, we've found that not every client can commit to a long enough call that allows for much detail, has the time to even schedule a monthly call, and some don't even want to do a monthly call, altogether.

So, these calls won't happen for every single client and for every single month. However, that's why I call it the ideal monthly review process with the goal of having as many clients as you possibly can commit to attending these calls.

Implement these monthly review calls consistently and it will significantly improve your retention rate. Your clients will feel pursued, know you truly care about their business, and know that you are working hard on a consistent basis to get them results.

It will give them the opportunity to see the results that you're generating while also building on your relationship.

Again, the number one reason the customer's going to leave is perceived indifference.

So if you're communicating with them at this level on a monthly, or at least quarterly, basis and you're sending them emails requesting a meeting or letting them know you tried to reach them three or four times, you'll be in a great place to have no reason for the client to leave you.

Tracking Retention

In any business, it's a proven fact that what gets measured gets done.

Naturally, you want to retain as many clients as you can, and you want to make sure that you're keeping most of them on board every month.

However, you need to have some type of metric in place which will be a key performance indicator for the health of your business.

So, I'm going to give you a tool to track your retention as you grow. Even if you're still on your first one, two, five, or 10 clients, you need to start tracking your retention rate if you are not already doing this.

As you measure your retention, you'll be able to realize if there is an issue and can take the necessary steps to improve it. You really can't build a successful marketing agency if you don't measure your client retention rate.

As I mentioned earlier, you won't retain clients if you don't provide great results coupled with an outstanding customer experience.

However, you won't know how well you're performing in either of these areas if you don't have some type of method for tracking and measuring your client retention rate.

Here is the formula for properly tracking your Client Retention Rate (CRR):

$$CRR = ((E-N)/S) *100$$

► E = Number of clients at the end of a period
► N = Number of new clients acquired during that period
► S = Number of clients at the start of that period

So, for example, let's say:

► E = Number of clients at the end of a period = 30
► N = Number of new clients acquired during that period = 5
► S = Number of clients at the start of that period = 28

The formula would be:

$$30 - 5 / 28 = 0.8928 \times 100 = 89.28\%$$

To monitor your client retention rate, you need to know the following 3 numbers at the end of any given period (for example, at the end of January):

► How many clients you have
► How many new clients you brought on during that period
► How many clients you had at the start of the period

With those three pieces of data, you can figure out what your retention rate is.

If the growth of your agency is important to you, then you must track and measure your client retention rate.

You can create a simple Excel spreadsheet with those numbers and track it on a monthly basis to create a basic customer retention tracking sheet. If the growth of your agency is important to you, and it should be, then you must create and use this spreadsheet to track and measure your client retention rate.

We talked at the beginning about setting goals and having a plan of attack to hit those goals. Tracking your client retention rate is an important part of this process.

I don't want it to seem like 100 percent retention is even feasible. It's going to be natural for about 5% to 8% of your customer base to cancel on any given month. That's just attrition, that's the way business goes.

However, the longer and more diligently you track these key performance indicators, the better you get at accomplishing your goals. Then, you can start to set higher, more ambitious goals and hit them because you're holding yourself accountable and you have a system in place on how to track it.

Again, the fundamental principle is that what gets measured gets done.

While you are using this tracking system, make sure not to overcomplicate it or feel like this is too simple for you to use. Just dive in and leverage it.

From an account management perspective, this entire client retention process also gives you the ability to be world-class within your niche.

So, make sure to follow all of the processes to develop and nurture your client relationships:

▶ Kick the relationship off on a solid basis so your client has positive feelings about you and your company
▶ Have a consistent strategy for communicating with your clients, showing them their results and then tracking your progress month by month

► Paint an exciting vision of what the future will look like, and communicate this vision to your client so they are encouraged to stay with you

Taking these 3 steps with each client, on a consistent basis, is really what's enabled us to average about a 97% monthly retention rate of our client base, which is high within our industry.

If you follow these steps, there's no reason you can't have the same results in your niche.

 SEVEN FIGURE ACTIONS

To take advantage of what you have learned in this chapter:

► Design a process to ensure you communicate to clients what you have planned for the next 30 to 90 days of their program

► Set up a spreadsheet to track your client retention rate

Case Study: Scale

A great example of a person who's scaled efficiently and effectively is Brian Stearman from Lawncare Marketing Mechanic.

A former police officer, Brian has been a member of ours for the past three years. He had run a lawncare business for a couple of years that had done well, and then sold it.

Then, Brian decided he was going to start a digital marketing agency serving the lawncare marketing world. He grew that relatively quickly to about $40,000 per month in recurring revenue but became quite bottlenecked.

The business was just him and his wife. He was the business development side, involved in all aspects of the company. She was helping with the website design, website structure, and website content piece of the equation.

Brian was aggressively adding three to five new clients every single month. They were starting to get stretched and just couldn't continue to do stay on top of the work.

He came to me and said, "Hey Josh, I think it's time for me to pause my sales and just focus on keeping things under control."

What I said is, "You know, Brian, you've got a unique opportunity. Your company's growing. There's a demand for what you do. A lot of people are trying hard to get to this place in their business where they've got some momentum going.

What you need to do is put some systems in place, and start to develop your team, so that you can continue to grow and scale.

You need to keep your foot on the gas instead of the brakes and work on building systems, procedures, and a team."

Fast-forward over the last year and a half and he's now at over $100,000 a month in recurring revenue. He was able to add about 19 clients in the last two or three months, and he was able to do this because he worked on developing systems, procedures, and a team.

Brian will tell you it hasn't been easy. He's trained, he's managed, he's hired, and he's fired.

He started by creating his organization chart and figuring out what he was best at and what he needed help with. Then Brian started to put people in place to help get the work done, so he wasn't doing it himself.

Brian's story is a great example of what's possible when you scale and free yourself up to grow while continuing to focus on sales and business development without doing all of the account management and customer support work yourself.

You can listen to a full interview with Brian Stearman on how he built and grew his agency by going to

https://www.sevenfigureagency.com/brian

10

FOLLOWING THE 7 FIGURE PATH

We started this book by talking about the Seven Figure Agency Model. We said there are three things you need to do. You need to:

- ▶ Land Clients
- ▶ Deliver Results
- ▶ Retain Clients Long-term

There are several things you need to consider to get the most out of this book:

- ▶ Your Business Model
  - o Will you choose to be a generalist or a specialist, serving a very specific niche?

o Will you continue to sell one-off project type work, or will you move to a recurring-only model?

o Will you decide on a core program with a monthly fee greater than $1K per month?

▶ How You Land Clients

o Will you continue to chase prospects, or will you put systems in place to get clients coming to you pre-positioned to buy?

o Will you commit to ongoing content development and leverage the ultimate content shortcut?

o Will you follow the consultative sales process and show clients exactly how you can help them and where their current strategy is deficient?

▶ How You Serve Your Clients And Get Them Results

o Will you commit to providing your clients a service/ program that provides tangible/measurable ROI or will you continue to offer activity-based services just for the sake of generating some income?

o Will you own the responsibility that as a business providing marketing services you are responsible for driving more leads, more sales and more growth for your clients?

▶ How You Retain Your Clients Long-term

o Will you put systems and processes in place to ensure your clients have an amazing onboarding experience?

o Will you ensure that you and your team communicate with them every step of the way and that they understand the value you are bringing to them?

o Will you go the extra mile to ensure your clients feel appreciated and pursued, and that they always see what's next and how you are going to continue taking them to the next level?

► How You Will Scale

   o   Will you try to do it all yourself or will you build a team around you?

   o   Will you leverage systems and procedures to ensure your team knows what is expected and can execute for your clients well and on a consistent basis?

Now that I've clarified all of these key areas, you now need to develop a plan. To get the most out of this book you can't just read it and walk away. You must now need to implement these strategies.

The Implementation Roadmap

7 Figure Agency - Business Plan

3 Years | Vision

12 Months | Goals

3 Months | Projects

This Week | Actions

We use a system called the Implementation Roadmap. You can download a copy from www.SevenFigureAgency.com/Kit, or you can just grab a blank sheet of paper and draw four boxes.

Spend a few minutes to get clear on what your three-year, 12-month and 90-day goals are.

► How many clients will you have and how much recurring revenue?

► What must you put in place to make this a reality?

Next, fill out your sales and retention tracking sheet, which you can download at: **www.sevenfigureagency.com/tracking**

Snap Shot	January Goal	Actual	Delta	February Goal	Actual	Delta	March Goal	A
Total Sales	7	5	-2	7	9	2	7	
Total Value	$13,300.00	$10,955.00	-$2,345.00	$13,300.00	$16,385.00	$3,085.00	$13,300.00	
Total Losses	3	7	4	3	6	3	3	
Value of Losses	$5,100.00	$10,000.00	$4,900.00	$5,100.00	$10,625.00	$5,525.00	$4,500.00	
Base Clients	136	134	-2	140	137	-3	144	
Base Revenue	$248,200.00	$242,905.00	-$5,295.00	$256,400.00	$248,665.00	-$7,735.00	$265,200.00	
Retention Rate	97.00%	95.56%	-1.44%	97.00%	95.52%	-1.48%	97.00%	
Net Growth	$6,200.00	$955.00			$5,760.00			

If you'd like to go deeper on these strategies and projects, then you should sign up for our Seven Figure Agency Roadmap LIVE™ workshop. We hold this event several times per year. For more information, go to: **www.SevenFigureAgencyBook.com**

If you can't make it to the live event, but are serious about growing and scaling your agency and want some help from me and my team, let's jump on an Agency Acceleration Session. Here is a link to schedule your session: **www.SevenFigureAgency.com/Schedule**

On this call, we will help you clarify the fastest path to grow and scale your agency. We'll also discuss how we can work together to help you implement the strategies outlined in this book to build the agency of your dreams.

That's all for now. Thank you for spending your precious time reading this book. I hope it has been of value to you and will propel you to bigger and better things in your business.

I wish you tremendous success and happiness and I look forward to meeting you in person, soon.

Josh Nelson

SPECIAL BONUS OFFER

Josh Nelson's Two-Day
Seven Figure Agency Roadmap LIVE
Workshop, Free!

As a special thank you for purchasing The Seven Figure Agency Roadmap, Josh Nelson is offering a scholarship for you and a team member to access The Seven Figure Agency Roadmap Implementation Training. That is a total value of $2,590 – for free!

This training is available to purchasers of Josh Nelson's The Seven Figure Agency Roadmap. This is a limited time offer and the workshop must be completed by the date shown on the following website at www. SevenFigureAgencyBook.com. There may be an administration fee or deposit taken upon registration, and this offer is made on a space availability basis. All seating is first-come, first-served.

To ensure your spot, please register immediately at www. SevenFigureAgencyBook.com.

At the Roadmap Live workshop, you will expand upon the insights provided in this book by learning how to:

- ► **Get More Clients**... By using client attraction methods that work without a marketing budget.
- ► **Profit from Serving Clients**... By productizing your service to increase profitability (in a way your clients will love).
- ► **Retain Clients for Life**... Without constantly spinning plates in the air, we'll fine tune your combination of recurring services and systems.
- ► **Create Your Desired Lifestyle**... By learning the right way to apply systems and teams to use your agency to create the life you want.

Here's What We'll Do Together at the Event...

- ▶ **Develop Your Irresistible Productized Offer** so you can immediately begin to serve clients more effectively and more profitably.

- ▶ **Implement Your Ultimate Agency Funnel** because we want you to leave with the tools already customized.

- ▶ **Install Your Client Attraction System** that increases lead flow and pre-sells clients on your value.

- ▶ **Learn to design the Team Templates that Create Leverage in Your Agency** which quickly aligns everyone on goals, values, and standards.

Register now by going to
www.sevenfigureagencybook.com